Growing Free

Growing Free

A

CARMELITE REMEMBERS

Sister Joan Williams, O.C.D.

ALBA · HOUSE　house　NEW · YORK

SOCIETY OF ST. PAUL, 2187 VICTORY BLVD., STATEN ISLAND, NEW YORK 10314

Library of Congress Cataloging-in-Publication Data

Williams, Joan, 1927-
  Growing Free.

  Bibliography: p.
    1. Williams, Joan, 1927-.   2. Carmelite Nuns —
  United States — Biography   I. Title.
  BX4705.W5595A3   1988   271'.97'024 [B]   87-30658
  ISBN 0-8189-0525-5

Designed, printed and bound in the United States of
America by the Fathers and Brothers of the
Society of St. Paul, 2187 Victory Boulevard,
Staten Island, New York 10314, as part of their
communications apostolate.

1 2 3 4 5 6 7 8 9 (Current Printing: first digit)

to

Miriam Elder, O.C.D and Anne Clem, O.C.D.

and to

all my Sisters and Brothers in Carmel

with

love and gratitude

CA
B
W

ACKNOWLEDGMENT

The sketch of Mt. Carmel by St. John of the Cross and the English translation of the terms used in it (pp. 42-43) are from *The Collected Works of St. John of the Cross*, translated by Kieran Kavanaugh, O.C.D. and Otilio Rodriguez, O.C.D. (Washington, DC: ICS Publications, 1979) and are used by permission of the publisher.

The stanza quoted on page 67 is from *"The Hollow Men"* in *Collected Poems 1909-1962* by T.S. Eliot, copyright 1936 by Harcourt Brace Jovanovich, Inc.; copyright © 1963, 1964 by T.S. Eliot Reprinted by permission of the publisher.

CONTENTS

INTRODUCTION

. . . silkworms feed on the mulberry-leaves
until they are full grown when they start
spinning silk, making themselves very tight
little cocoons. Finally, the worm, which was
large and ugly, comes out of the cocoon a
beautiful white butterfly.

St. Teresa of Avila

This is a story about a Carmelite nun.

A story about opposites:
    about darkness and light,
    about desert and water.

A story about desire —
    a butterfly cocooned in desires,
    a bird held by a slender thread.

    This is a story about growing free.

Part I

IN THE MULBERRY LEAVES

1

FIRST MEMORIES

My first "whole picture" memory is a bright tableau. The sun directly overhead, everything dry and white and glaring. My sisters, Jane and Peggy, stand near Johnny, our cook. Rexie, our dog, black with white front, stands, too, at rigid attention. Then the tableau comes to life. Everyone talks at once, pointing to the nearby wooden bridge that crosses the little creek behind our house. Now I see the snake. It is quite dead and so big it hangs from the bridge railing in two fluid gray-green loops. I race from the bridge to the creek to see where the snake has been killed. Johnny loudly calls after me, "Come back!" But it is too late. My sandals are already soaked, my flowered cotton dress splashed with mud.

Later, after the excitement was over, I stood meekly in the slippery tub, my small fingers clutching Johnny's strong black arm while she gently scolded me. The youngest, at four, I enjoyed a certain immunity when it came to scoldings, especially Johnny's. I loved Johnny with all my small heart. She combined warmth and dignity in her ample frame. Standing straight, and from my limited vantage point, tall, she moved around in this affectionate atmosphere of our home like a sailboat, apron billowing about her, overseeing, cooking and generally maintaining order among us all.

My mother, Julia McDonough, was born in Cincinnati's Price Hill and grew up there. My father, Thomas Williams, was from Covington. I was born in 1927 at St. Joseph's Infirmary, in Louisville, when mother was twenty-nine. My sister, Jane, ten years older than I, was a dark, curly-headed, vivacious child. Peggy Lynn came next, my blue-eyed, blond sister, intrigued by all of life and old enough at five to be especially intrigued by the new baby.

Shortly after my birth, Dad was asked to be president of a Chicago firm. On the train, enroute to Chicago, with all of us, he received a telegram informing him of the company's collapse, an omen of the approaching Great Depression. We stayed a year in Chicago and then returned to Louisville. It was to be the first of many moves.

We were a very close-knit family even though my parents led an active social life. I remember, even as a small child, being aware of the extraordinary closeness between my parents. Sometimes it had struck me as strange for grown-ups to hug and laugh so much. I sensed, even at places like the breakfast table, deep currents of feeling passing between them, making them one. Their knowing glances over my head and cryptic remarks in no way escaped me, but the import was certainly lost. Probably because I was the youngest, I was often tucked between them in our family Ford and off we'd go together, to visit friends. On the way home, even though half asleep, I could hear the crickets' sound, whirring, whirring through the car windows. Nothing could have made me feel any happier or safer.

I remember, too, the anticipation I felt when the shimmer of Mother's evening gown, or the white front of Dad's tuxedo appeared at the door of my room. They brought to my sisters and me tid-bits from their parties, stashed away in pocket or purse: chocolates, hors d'oeuvres or lace-edged petits fours — all capped by a final comforting tucking-in kiss.

Ours was a reading family and I loved to be read to. I remember Mother lying on her chaise longue, book in hand, or Dad sitting in his chair reading in the evening. We grew up in a book-filled house where the Harvard Classics sat next to Grimm's Fairy Tales. They in turn were neighbors to poetry, books on equine jumping and human anatomy. My father had once planned to be a doctor when young. We children read in every conceivable situation: eating, walking, riding on the bus, in bed, and for me (when I learned to read) under the bed covers with a flashlight after my bedtime had passed.

I went everywhere with my parents — they even took me to the Derby. I can still feel the wire pressing against my legs when my father held me up to see the lead pony. The horses came out shaking their heads, snorting and side-stepping — their jockeys in colored silks, whip in hand. I was given a program, even though I couldn't read it, and chose the name of "my" horse, my bet placed with the others. I watched, breathless, as each horse was led to the starting gate. Suddenly there was the roar of hooves, the louder roar of the crowd and the announcer's voice hammering out the position of the horses. Then the winner crossed the line. I never tired of the races, though when the day was over my eyes refused to stay open.

Both my mother and my sister, Jane, often won trophies at horse shows. When they were first married, my father learned to ride so that he could be with Mother when she rode in shows. He felt it the proper thing to do. He told me once how an old German riding instructor had made him sit for hours straddling a wooden horse to learn "how to sit your horse properly." The fact that my father persevered in this effort was typical of him. If he was going to do something, he wanted to do it "right." In my fascination with horses I wanted to ride, too. When the day came for my first try, I was placed on our fat brown and white pony, Lady. We had a horse, as I remember, but that was for the grown-ups. Once on Lady's back, I looked down and my feet seemed far from the ground. Overcome with fear as Lady moved forward, I dropped the reins and hung onto her mane, tearfully demanding to be taken off. From then on, I left the riding to Mother and my sisters. My parents never pushed us children to excel in any particular way. They were content to let us develop at our own pace, though, by this time, each of them in their own realm had obtained a certain measure of success.

When I was six, we moved from Louisville to Cincinnati where my father was to be sales manager for Philco Tri-State Distributing Corporation. Moving was hard for everyone. The canary drooped, Rex followed us around with cocked head and a puzzled look in her eyes, Johnny cried into her apron, and I cried on general principles. My father promised Johnny that he would send for her as soon as we were settled. I stood around watching Peggy and Jane help mother pack our belongings into big cardboard boxes, fearful my toys would be lost. The next thing I knew we had moved into our apartment on Erie Avenue. Having outgrown much of my early timidity, I quickly adjusted to city life, running around the complex with the other children, ringing doorbells and dashing away. At first I missed our pretty little white stucco house in the Louisville suburbs with its creek and wooden bridge in the back. Within the year we had a house in Hyde Park. To my joy Johnny came back, and all was well.

Mother Leaves Us

IN 1935, the year after our move to Arcadia Place, my parents went to a convention in Florida, a combined business and pleasure trip. I remember the details clearly. Mother developed pneumonia when she returned in February to Cincinnati's cold. Our family doctor came to see her daily, but her condition become steadily worse. There were no antibiotics in those days. Johnny no longer sang as she worked and we all tiptoed about uncertainly. Then one day an ambulance arrived. I watched from the living room windows as Mother's white covered form was carried away. Peggy, who was twelve, put her arm around me and said, "She'll be back." Filled with a child's nameless terror, "No," I replied, "she won't come back." I remained crying at the window for a long time. I was a small deserted fledgling.

A few days later, I found Dad inside sitting on the steps, his head in his hands. The picture in my fairytale book of the Prince sitting beneath a tree in a dark forest, a spell upon him, came to me. I had never seen Dad cry before and I knew instinctively that Mother was dead. Horrified, I crept past him to my room. I couldn't fathom what death meant. The fact of Mother's death floated meaningless, unresolved on the shallow pond of my consciousness. Further information — Mother would be buried — made ever-widening circles of unreadable images. What was happening? What did it mean, to die? To be buried? Hushed preparations for the funeral began. I was not taken to the wake or funeral Mass. Dad wanted me to remember Mother as she had been in life, not to have a last memory of her as a still, silent face.

I have remembered Mother, but only in a child's pattern of vivid colors, the feel of touch and sensations: her shining black hair, enormous blue eyes, ivory white skin, the light touch of her fingers anchoring my crib blankets with huge safety pins . . . in later years how she hugged me to herself, saying I was not too big to sit on her lap, though at six my legs dangled to the floor like a giant rag doll's. At seven, I had only a child's memories to call on. Mother had always been present and a tomorrow without her was unthinkable. Time for me, as yet, had nothing to do with

clocks. It was all, as Henri Bergson said, duration, a round ball
held easily in my small hands. I was protected in a certain
measure by my ignorance of what life and death meant, encased
as I was by my child's unknowing. Later, and little by little,
memory crystallized these first seven years: then I could hold
them to the light, hear the sound of Mother's voice, see the two
of us, even catch again the fragrance of her perfume.

The morning after the funeral, my father, Peggy, Jane and I
sat in desolate silence in the bright dining room trying to eat
breakfast. I began to sob into my Wheaties. Dad said that
Mother's death was very hard on all of us, but that I, especially,
must be a strong soldier. Given his own overpowering grief, it
was probably the best advice he could muster at the time, but it
was little comfort for me. I needed something more, but at the
time no one realized how deeply affected I was by Mother's
death. My fear of the dark increased and I often woke, screaming, from terrible nightmares.

Mother's side of the family, the fervently Catholic
McDonoughs, did try to help me. They painted glowing word
pictures about life after death. Aunt Mabel said, with complete
conviction shining in her brown eyes, that Mother was with God
in heaven and would never suffer again. I had overheard Jane
talking about Mother's illness, how her arms had been covered
with bruises from I.V.'s, so I had the scary realization that
Mother had suffered — and was vastly relieved to know that she
wouldn't suffer anymore. The fact that Mother would always be
happy didn't impress me. After all, I thought, we had all been
happy together. The part I liked best was when Aunt Mabel
insisted that Mother loved me still and would always watch over
me. My nightmares lessened and I wasn't quite as afraid at night,
though I still carried out a quick ritual check for any foreign
beings under my bed or behind the organdy curtains. Quickly,
because I was never sure if I wanted to know whether something
was there or not. By the time spring came I was calmer, though I

still missed Mother greatly. The jonquils she had loved bloomed in the garden; in a fit of anger, I walked on them. How dare they come back without Mother?

Dad said he was a Protestant, a fact backed by a tintype picture of him as an infant robed in yards of baptismal white. Though he never attended church services of any kind, he was exceptionally faithful in honoring his marriage promise, making sure that we children went to Mass and Catholic schools. Now, as I look back, I think he saw this as part of his fidelity to Mother. Every night he laid aside his reading — he read constantly and had a large library of cherished books — and patiently went over my catechism with me in preparation for my First Communion. Often, to my delight, he would talk about other things as well: about his youth, which I thought must have been years and years ago, although he was only in his forties. Sometimes he reminisced about Mother. "Your mother was a beautiful woman, the most beautiful woman I'd ever seen. She and Cecile McDevitt shared an informal title: 'Cincinnati's Two Most Beautiful Women.' When we met, Jule was eighteen and I was twenty-one. She was with Walter Vester and I was with another girl. But when I saw Jule, I said to myself, 'This is the girl I'm going to marry.' We were married the next year. Neither Jule nor I gave a thought to all those suitors left behind, but I never forgot how lucky I was." Holding my hands, he would absent-mindedly stroke my fingers saying, "Your mother's fingers were long and tapered." I would try on his special ring, a diamond Mother's father had given her when she came of age. One year, as a surprise for Dad, Mother had had the stone reset — we children excitedly contributing our piggy-bank savings for the setting. Such moments of closeness and shared memories helped to heal my hurt.

After Mother died, Grandma came to live with us, Rebecca Green Williams. Small in stature, she nonetheless radiated a gracious dignity. She had silver gray hair, and always wore a black velvet ribbon around her throat, her twinkly blue eyes framed by steel-rimmed glasses. Always carefully dressed, she usually wore a black satin skirt, a white blouse, the ruchings held in place by a silver mourning pin. This pin contained a single curl of her only daughter's hair. Margaret died at sixteen. Grandma was a symbol for me of steadfastness, a loving presence that was always there — and mine. I was delighted, as we all were, when Grandma came, for she was a special favorite. She made us cookies, she made us taffy, she knitted by the fire and gave me a tiny black kitten to play with. She also raised canaries, but most of all, she raised our spirits by giving us this healing time of peace and love.

After my father, Grandma was the most significant person in my life. She had a wonderful way of always telling the truth with gentleness. Seated one day at her dressing table, I studied my face carefully in the mirrors, a little pinched-looking face with glasses, framed by straight brown hair. I had heard innumerable times about Mother's great beauty. Wistfully, I asked, "Grandma, am I beautiful?" She laid down her knitting and looked at me thoughtfully. "You have a very patrician face," she replied. I wasn't quite sure what it meant, but it sounded wonderful — I was thrilled.

I always picture Grandma sitting in her rocker by the big window in her living room. She is holding either a newspaper or a book, the rings on her hands catching the light. Peggy, when I was still quite small, had taught me to read with the funny papers. I always wanted to know why she was laughing. I was crazy about books and wanted to read everything. I read not only children's books at home, but anything else that caught my fancy. The results were sometimes hilarious. One day Grandma complained with uncharacteristic vehemence about my mother's cousin, a frequent visitor. I said very solemnly, "Don't worry, Grandma, she's just a harlot." I knew something was wrong when I saw her look of astonishment. She gasped a bit and asked carefully, "Honey Heart, where did you hear that word?" "I read it in the Bible, but I didn't know what it meant so I looked it up in the dictionary." "And what did the dictionary say?" "It said that a harlot is a woman of bad character, and that's what *she* is." Grandma had to take off her glasses to wipe away tears of laughter. She cautioned me never to use that word again. Since I was working on my vocabulary, I didn't know how I was going to obey. I had to use each new word three times — and I still had two to go.

Mother's death had taken its toll of my father's health. Day by day he seemed to change from the father I knew into an older version of the slender, brown-haired young man of the pictures in our old family album. He didn't seem to notice me, or any of us, though in his loneliness, I saw he welcomed the visits of my mother's married cousin, Marjorie. Marge was a striking woman. I was a little afraid of her. With her olive skin, hazel eyes and short black hair, swept back from a high forehead, she looked very sophisticated and remote to me. Larry, her four-year-old son, had blond hair with a marked cow-lick, blue eyes, and still carried an endearing amount of baby fat. We studied each other from a safe distance. From the time of Mother's funeral, Marge and Larry were a presence in our house. I didn't realize then what was happening, that soon she was to be my new step-mother. At the time I just accepted her visits without question. Later, during my teens, I pieced together the story of her difficult life.

After she left college, Marge married. It was to be a strained relationship. She was often lonely because her pharmacist husband worked long hours at her father's drugstore. Even the arrival of Larry, her first and only child, didn't help for, as she told Hilda, his nurse, partly in jest, partly in earnest, "Take him away and bring him back when he has some sense."

Although Marge's first marriage slowly disintegrated, she did not divorce her husband until her mother, a devout

Catholic, died. Her mother's death was a turning point. Marge insisted she could no longer believe in a God who let innocent people suffer. A crisis of faith followed during which she regularly consulted Monsignor Wagner, a friend of her family. His reassurance failed, and her collapse of faith, along with her general unhappiness, led to her divorce. When the divorce was finalized, she married my father.

Unfortunately, her second marriage wasn't too happy either. I overheard the constant arguments that broke out between Marge and my sisters, and my harried father trying to calm things down. I realized later that Marge, in her mid-thirties, found an eighteen-year-old step-daughter an embarrassment, and a thirteen-year-old, a nuisance. Younger than my two sisters, I watched everything with a child's fear and uncertainty. The secure and untroubled world I had known with my parents was crumbling at an alarming rate. A few months after Marge and Dad married, Johnny was sent away, Grandma was moved to an apartment in Covington, and my two sisters were sent to Brown County, a boarding school run by the Ursuline nuns. It was understood that Sundays were spent with Peggy and Jane. Dad, Marge, Larry and I would all pile in the car for the fifty mile drive to Brown County. We always went to the old country inn near school for a noon dinner of their famous fried chicken and biscuits. About five we would drive back to school. Often at home on week-days, I would stand by the phone in Dad's study while he called Peggy and Jane, waiting for my turn to say hello. Sometimes he called me to his desk so that I could add my scribble to his weekly letter.

Mother and Dad had gone out a great deal socially, but with Marge's coming an endless round of dinner parties and dances began. Neither Larry, my step-brother, nor I, minded being left alone with the current cook, but I missed the times my father and I used to spend together. Now, Marge was always there. I felt she usurped my place, and I blamed her in part for the fact that my grandmother and sisters were no longer at home. I made special plans to see how I could be alone with Dad. I waited at the front door to say goodbye in the morning and in the evening walked to the head of our street to ride part way back with him.

After a difficult period of adjustment (now *he* was the baby), Larry and I joined forces. We learned that we could count on the cooks. We had a series of cooks for they, too, had to contend with Marge's troublesome times. Vivian was one of our favorites, though we feared her tongue-lashings when we tracked mud in the house, or didn't pick up our clothes. We took Vivian with us to Michigan one summer, to a cabin at Klinger Lake. One afternoon as a special favor, she made lemonade and sandwiches for my friend and me, though it was past lunch time. I threw my arms around her in a hug of gratitude. One of the adults remarked, "Joan, you don't thank the help for doing what they are paid to do." This was my first rude awakening to the world of race and prejudice. Though so young, I burned with embarrassment for Vivian and deeply resented such unkindness. I couldn't at all understand how such good people could be so cruel.

As I grew older my relationship with Marge went through various stages. My first stage was one of confusion. An affectionate child, I wanted to be loved. What I experienced from Marge was a puzzling combination of love and rejection. Her first cocktails of the evening produced a loving reaction to which I enthusiastically responded, chattering away about my books and friends, desperate to make the most of such precious time. However, with the second and third martini, Marge's affectionate remarks became carping. She would correct me for not being in my room, or scold me for being unable to report properly about whatever book I was reading, Beethoven's life, for example, and the date of the Ninth Symphony. Her behavior gradually became understandable to me as I realized she had a drinking problem. And, later still, I realized besides this, that Marge was not at peace with herself. When she took me with her to visit her mother's grave, and in tears told me about her mother, and her goodness, I realized that at such times, Marge saw the shambles of her own life through her mother's eyes. Part of the torment Marge lived with, it seems to me now, stemmed from her denial of a faith which wasn't really dead, but remained alive in a sort of superstitious fear and guilt. Marge had gotten what she wanted, but was tormented by its possession. I wanted to help her then, but had no idea of what to do.

Marge's religious problems and difficulties colored much of life at home. For example, in spite of her ridicule, my father, a naturally religious man, knelt down every night in his pajamas by the side of his bed to say his prayers. I wanted to be like him, to say my prayers, too, and hold fast to my religion. My faith at that time was devotion to my father, as much as to the Father. In fact, for me God was just a bigger and better Father. As I grew older, I did begin to see that Dad wasn't quite as "perfect" as I had thought — he had his faults, too. For some reason, I never blamed him for my difficult life with Marge. I guess I felt sorry for him.

Though I had begun to understand better Marge's problems, I wasn't mature enough emotionally to know how to handle the situation. I continued to hope that someday Marge would accept me. When all my efforts failed, I finally rebelled. I was fourteen by then and in the midst of my adolescent upheavals. I rebelled and went to opposite extremes in my behavior. The slightest criticism or hint of disapproval from Marge or anyone brought on an outburst of tears and angry words. I used to lie on my bed in my white and gold room, moodily wondering what life would have been like if Mother had lived. My unhappiness grew, fueled by a religion teacher who constantly told us "how grateful you should be to have been born." I felt anything but grateful. I said to myself over and over again, "I never asked to be born." I envied my friends' peaceful family life. I did not know why Dad stayed with Marge, but I was aware that nothing would ever change. My sense of despair and of being trapped increased. This despair and darkness was very real, but they did not dampen my youthful exuberance. I somehow managed to enjoy, between the emotional upheavals at home and my own problems, all the normal teen-age activities: pretty clothes, dating, dancing, parties.

I visited Grandma Williams on weekends and in summer, and I went with my sisters to art galleries, movies and plays. Sororities and teas were all part of this helter-skelter growing-up period. One date is indelibly imprinted on my mind. It was December 7, 1941. Four of us, riding in a blue convertible, were on our way to a sorority meeting, the radio blaring. Suddenly the music stopped. Pearl Harbor had been bombed. We were part of a war that up to then had been mostly unreal to me. One girl started to cry, "My brother will have to go." As the months passed, the war came closer. The brother of Jeanne, my roommate at Brown County, was to take me to a Christmas Eve dance. An airforce pilot, he was shot down over Burma and listed as missing in action. Instead of going to a dance, I went to his memorial service.

Though others gave so much, we were not a patriotic family. The war changed my values, but not through any personal deprivation. Marge saw to it that our cellar was full of canned fruit, ham and vegetables. We saved gas coupons from both cars and made our usual trip to Virginia Beach. The only problem during our trip occurred when driving through the five o'clock traffic rush in Washington. The muffler fell off our blue Chrysler. We roared through the Capitol with all its signs and posters asking, "Is this trip really necessary?" Filled with teen-age embarrassment (why did my family always have to be different?), I shrank into the corner of the back seat, trying to become invisible.

The Virginia Beach place where we stayed was a huge white frame building several stories high. I especially remember the old-fashioned veranda that fronted on the sea. After dinner we often sat there with the other guests, watching the big war ships go by. One evening, the people in the suite opposite us had an impromptu cocktail party. A slender black-haired man called to me as I passed to go to my room, "Come and have a drink with us." I was surprised, because though no longer a child, there was still a great gap between what I did and what my parents did. I replied cautiously, "No thanks." As I walked away I heard a female voice say in an annoyed tone, "You fool, she's only fifteen." I was flattered nonetheless. My sudden exposure to life outside Hyde Park was proving very exciting.

College boys had most of the summer jobs at the hotel. As I came to breakfast the morning after our arrival, one of them was waiting for me. He said in well-worn words that were new and intriguing to me, "As soon as you walked in the door, I knew I wanted to meet you. What do you like to do? What do you want to see?" We swam together a few times and walked hand in hand along the beach. Gardenias bloomed outside the door — it was wonderful. "Have you," he asked, "ever seen the moon come up over the ocean?" I admitted that I hadn't. His description of this phenomenon was so impressive that I immediately agreed to meet him on the veranda at midnight. What a lark! (Like sitting on the fire escape and smoking.) For me, a date usually meant going to well-chaperoned sorority dances where boys had the same rigorous standards of behavior as girls. So I arrived promptly, and unsuspectingly, to see the moon rise. We sat on the swing — I left a careful distance between us. The gap was instantly filled and I found myself in a warm embrace. Suddenly, I realized what his real intentions were. "Listen," I said furiously, "I came here to see the moon, not for this." With as much hauteur as I could muster — and speed, I stood up and declared I was leaving. His anger equalled my own. He shouted after me, "I'll tell everyone what a dud you are — you won't have any friends. The rest of us will all be at parties and you'll be all alone." This proved to be true. I saw him often on the beach, the center of a laughing group, but I didn't care — I was so glad to have escaped unscathed.

The war was very real here at Virginia Beach. When I walked along the boardwalk the big guns were always there, posted at regular intervals, pointing menacingly out to sea. When we were driving, we often had to pull over to let army convoys of soldiers pass. I began to think a lot about life and about death. Many of these boys would shortly face death. What was I doing with my life?

When we got home from Virginia Beach that fall, my father ceremoniously gave me my own front door key, with a list of what I considered childish restrictions. However, it was definitely a step in the right direction. My key offered new possibilities; I was almost on my own. I learned, also, to drive my best friend's car. Claire and I were next door neighbors. We used to take the car out on country roads, going as fast as we could. Unfortunately, the Oldsmobile speedometer had a way of sticking at seventy so we could never be sure of our speed. This same famous car was used for our end-of-war celebration. When word came over the radio of the Hiroshima bombing, our crowd, laughing and screaming, threw our gas coupons away, and got the tank filled. None of us realized the horror of nuclear bombs and what the future would hold. The war was over. The future was a world of peace.

Ah, Bright Wings

INTO my confused growing-up world of sun and shadow, came another kind of light, a pure gift from God. I began to be aware of Christ's presence, an infinitely comforting Presence. I was not alone, Someone cared. I experienced a certain peace. Religion became real to me. It was no longer something I simply read or heard about or a question of imitating what my father did. I experienced God in my life in a new and deeper way. In this strange new peace that was mine, I tasted again the sweet honeysuckle blossoms of my early childhood, I felt the warm earth and the heavy summer air that had carried Mother's call.

In my second year at the Ursuline boarding school, where I, too, had been sent, Peggy gave me *The Imitation of Christ* and *The New Testament* bound in one volume. I took it everywhere. This "conversion" however, continued to be a slightly mixed experience. Far from leaving everything "worldly" behind, I wanted the best of both worlds. For instance, reading novels was still a favorite pastime. One day at school I wandered into a section of the library, "off limits to students." Hoping to find something romantic by D.H. Lawrence or Henry Miller, I found to my surprise, the works of the mystics. Apparently, the sister in charge was concerned that we were too impressionable to read them. I ran my fingers over the books, pulling out St. Gertrude, whose name I recognized, and other large volumes on prayer that meant nothing to me. For no particular reason, I chose *The Autobiography of St. Teresa of Avila*, and, for good measure, took the book next to it, *The Ascent of Mount Carmel* by St. John of the Cross. I discovered that these saints both belonged to the Order of Carmel.

I ultimately read all of St. Teresa's books, quietly slipping into the library when no one was around. Her *Way of Perfection* captured my heart. She was writing for *me*. The orderly progression of *The Interior Castle* fascinated me as much as St. Teresa's constant digressions describing her friends, her health, her travels, her business transactions. I read during study hours, at recreation, during any free time. I was fascinated by the fact that her background was very much like my own. Her mother had died when she was young, she had had a worldly cousin (I had my cousin Cece) who led her a bit astray. Like me, she turned to the Blessed Virgin and in her found a Mother. She was fond of clothes and jewelry — fond even of reading novels. Things were looking up. St. Teresa's practicality and good humor, and her tremendous vitality appealed to me greatly. She was a vivid, down-to-earth woman.

Her words about prayer jumped out of the pages to me in an *aha!* experience. "Since you are alone, the first thing you must do is look for a friend." I felt I had found my spiritual home. "In order," she wrote, "to ascend to the dwelling places we desire, the important thing is not to think much but to love much. . . ." In my own fumbling way, I tried to follow her directions for prayer. I was deeply impressed by St. Teresa's example, by the frankness with which she owned her faults — and how she anticipated the problems that come with a life of prayer — dryness, distractions, and the always-present temptation to give up prayer completely. I loved her happy, exuberant personality.

I did not have long periods for prayer, but because of the joy I felt in the presence of the Blessed Sacrament, I made short visits to the school chapel between classes. I was experiencing an ever-growing sense of Christ's presence and encouragement.

A great and unbounded enthusiasm for prayer marked this period of my life. However, I had no judgment or real experience or discernment in spiritual ways. I had no notion of what St. John of the Cross meant when he said that the experience of God's favors was not the experience of God himself. God's consolations and God were the same things as far as I was concerned. In fact, I found all of St. John of the Cross difficult to understand.

One of the most glaring examples of my massive naivete showed itself when I informed the chaplain that in reading St. Teresa's *Interior Castle*, it seemed to me I was in the Third Mansion.* He managed not to laugh and suggested I find a spiritual director for guidance in such serious reading. This idea pleased me, for St. Teresa had spoken of the need for spiritual direction as had St. John of the Cross.

It was much easier to pray at school than at home, I discovered. That summer, when I was on my own, I made more or less valiant attempts to attend daily Mass, but nothing ever interfered with my parties — and dancing to the music of Glenn Miller, Benny Goodman and Harry James. I found a sort of guilty consolation in the thought that St. Teresa in her young years had had similar struggles between a strong attraction to prayer and to worldliness. In moments of insight, I became aware of the contrast between my life at school and my life at home. With typical adolescent righteousness, however, I began to criticize not my own lifestyle, but that of Dad and Marge. Their life seemed empty and meaningless. I began to think I should do something meaningful with my life. This desire for a meaningful life, coupled with the reading of St. Teresa, gradually convinced me that only a life of prayer could fulfill my longing to reach out to others and to help everyone. Carmel, I thought, would satisfy my thirst for the Absolute. I wanted to sacrifice everything — the good and the "bad." I thought that in the monastery I would no longer be tempted by invitations to parties and dances, movies and sports. Carmel would offer the solitude, silence and penance I wanted and felt were necessary for prayer. It was a grand vision! I felt I was being called to an adventure beyond anything I had dreamed of — a journey into the Unknown. Though I had made up my mind to be a Carmelite, I didn't know if there were any Carmels in the United States, indeed, if the Order was still in existence.

In my Junior year, when I was sixteen, the school retreat*   was given by Father Wernert, a Jesuit priest. In confession, I told him I wanted to be a Carmelite. He was delighted with the idea of directing a contemplative vocation. He gave me a time and a date during my Easter vacation to come and see him. He was Dean of Men at Xavier University in Cincinnati. I went home at the end of every month, so, after that, once a month I visited Father Wernert. During one of these visits, he gave me a book with an abbreviated history of Carmel, a sort of fact sheet: The name, "Carmel" came from Mt. Carmel in the Holy Land where the order originated. The rule was written in the early 1200s. After the fall of the Kingdom of Jerusalem, the Order spread into the West. Two sixteenth century Spanish saints, Teresa of Avila and John of the Cross, led a reform in the Carmelite Order resulting in another branch of the family tree. Membership of each monastery of nuns was limited to a small number. The life was strictly cloistered and devoted to prayer, silence and solitude. It wasn't much information, but it was enough for me.

Convinced that I was serious about my vocation, Father Wernert gave me the addresses of those Carmels closest to Cincinnati, Louisville, Cleveland and Indianapolis. I wrote only to Indianapolis. Mother Agnes replied and our correspondence began. No one else knew of my plan. One weekend when I was home from school, my father met me at the door, an unopened letter from Mother Agnes in his hand. He demanded to know what it meant. Although he may have suspected the possibility of my vocation, when he actually saw the return address of a Carmelite Monastery he was deeply disturbed. I told him then that I was seriously thinking of entering. More stern than I had ever seen him, he said that absolutely nothing was to be done until I had finished a year of college. I had never argued with my father before and the feeling of now being apart from him, and alone, was overwhelming.

Dear Mother Agnes,

My Confessor has suggested that since I have an inclination toward joining the Carmelite order I write to you and ask for some information. Perhaps you could tell me some certain line of reading matter also, that I could follow?

I am sixteen now and I will graduate next year.

Sincerely,

Joan Williams

July the fifth

Mother Agnes, in one of her letters, invited me to come to Indianapolis for Sister Marian's Veiling Ceremony.* Dad agreed to let me go, thinking that if I saw what Carmelite life was like, I would change my mind. Claire came with me. From Union Terminal, with its famous mosaics, we took the Riley train to Indianapolis. It was mobbed with young soldiers eager to strike up conversations. One asked us where we were going. I didn't say to a monastery.

After the ceremony, with some trepidation, I went by myself to the parlor to meet, for the first time, Mother Agnes and the novice-mistress, Mother Miriam. After the first few awe-struck seconds, I was soon telling them all about myself. Mother Agnes asked me if I thought I could learn to obey. I replied blithely, that of course I could. Now I wonder if I had any idea at all of what obedience meant. After I left the parlor, I thought of all the questions I should have asked! Afterwards, Claire and I lingered in the monastery, enjoying the faint fragrance of incense and the total silence. I kept wondering about the people *inside*; it was totally beyond anything I had ever experienced. I might as well have been in some far distant world. While I could hardly believe that I had a vocation to this beautiful life, I felt an immense and driving desire to enter it, its very mystery carrying me along in an irresistible current. Claire and I were entranced, looking at everything about us, seeing through the soft filtered light, the Romanesque arches, the iron grilles, and Our Lady's statue. Walking along the outside of the building, we pointed out to each other the fossils in the Kentucky riverbottom stone and traced them with our fingers. I came away with a new determination to be a Carmelite.

When I returned home, filled with enthusiasm for Carmel, Dad's hopes were disappointed. We had bitter arguments about my vocation. He enrolled me at the University of Kentucky. To prove my independence, I got a summer job, my first, as a nurse's aide at the Children's Convalescent Home. I had applied at several places, but gladly accepted this job because it tied in with the reading in psychology I had begun the summer before. I had then gone to the library and unabashedly asked a puzzled librarian where to find the works of Carl Jung, pronounced with a "J" as in John, and Freud, pronounced as in the word, "feud." I loved the work with the children and was good at it. During any free time we had we were allowed to read the children's case histories. In some of them I found cases of child abuse which I never dreamed existed. In less serious times my immaturity manifested itself by my singing and dancing through the wards to amuse the children — until firmly corrected by the supervisor. Nonetheless, this same supervisor offered to send me through nurse's training if I would, later, work there. My resolve to be a Carmelite remained unchanged, though I was flattered and pleased by her proposal.

My continued resolve to enter Carmel ran parallel with an equally strong resolve to have as much fun as possible before entering the convent. To celebrate my first paycheck, my cousin Cece suggested we meet at the Music Box, an attractive little downtown bar in the Fountain Square Hotel. She was not much older than myself, but infinitely more sophisticated. We drank Pink Ladies the rest of the afternoon. I had been complaining to her that since Father Wernert had been transferred to Milford as novice master, I had no spiritual director. Cece suggested that on the way home we see a friend of her family's, Father Kallaher.

Before leaving the Music Box, Cece and I made our slightly unsteady way to the restroom. One door said "Altos," one "Sopranos." "I can sing alto," said Cece. We somehow managed the streetcar, though we hadn't much balance left. Stumbling up the steps of St. Mary's Rectory we rang the doorbell. A grim-faced housekeeper with iron-gray hair pulled back in a tight knot opened the door. We asked to see Father Kallaher. In icy tones, she said, "His Reverence is not in." While we stood absorbing this news, she added, pointedly, "I suggest you come back, another day." With that, she firmly shut us out.

My seventeenth summer was to be my last "in the world" and I made the most of it. I lay in a deck chair by the pool at Hyde Park Country Club in a two-piece bathing suit, drinking coke and seriously explaining my vocation to friends. The incongruity of it didn't strike me for years.

I had the usual teen romances, all part of the "normal existence" Father Wernert suggested! I went everywhere for a while, with a man in his twenties who wanted to marry me. One night, when he and I were standing together in our hall before a large oval mirror and looking at our reflection, I suddenly realized that for me marriage was not the answer. He was hurt and angry. I was confused, but sure, still in some dark way, of my true vocation.

My father was puzzled. I seemed to be leading a "normal life," yet I seemed to remain serious about Carmel. We both, independently, checked out the legal situation and found there was no law to prevent me from entering at eighteen. Dad finally yielded. He wanted me to be happy, but still felt deeply that I was "throwing away" my life.

Mother Agnes, aware of my father's disapproval, invited him to visit the Indianapolis monastery. From my own visit there with Claire, I knew what was coming. We had laughed at the grates and grilles, even though we were impressed, but I hadn't prepared my father. I didn't know what to say even as we walked slowly up the stone steps to the massive oak door. The door had hand-wrought iron bars and hinges, and above it was the carved stone Seal of Carmel*. My father said gently, "Don't you think you'd better put out your cigarette?" In my nervousness, I had forgotten I was still holding it. We pushed open the door. It creaked and groaned in the best tradition of all spooky places. As we entered, the first thing we saw was the dimly illumined carving of St. Thérèse lying on her catafalque, cross and roses clasped in her arms. It didn't help matters.

Ordinarily in complete control of every situation, my father looked dazed. He rang the bell and we waited. Light filtered down from above us. As we stood in the soft light we heard footsteps, and a voice through a black curtained window in the wall called, "Deo gratias, is someone there, please?" We identified ourselves and were given directions to the speak room.

The speak room, or parlor, was divided in the middle by two sets of grilles, upright rods first and lattice work behind, all of it iron. We were on one side, the nuns on the other. The lattice had black curtains and behind the curtains were shutters. We heard the sharp click of bolts being released and saw light behind.

I sat beside my father, miserable and wondering what he thought. To my relief, Mother Agnes pulled back the grate curtains and she and Mother Miriam raised their veils. Mother Agnes had rosy cheeks and great blue eyes and both nuns were young. I felt my father relax. These were normal, pleasant people, not wasted penitential-looking creatures. They both seemed to understand my father's feelings. Their whole manner held a happy ordinariness. I felt my father's resistance begin to weaken. With relief I heard him ask, "Joan doesn't drink coffee, will she be able to have cocoa?" There was a choice of coffee or cocoa for breakfast. (I found later that "ours" however, was a special brand of chocolate made with water and thickened with clippings from the altar breads. The coffee was "stretched" with chicory.) I was relieved when the visit was over. We went to the Athletic Club for lunch with two of my father's business friends. I thought it a good sign that, when cocktails were ordered, my father chose a special sherry for me.

As Dad's objections lessened, and it became evident that I was going to get my way, I began to have second thoughts. I had fought so long for Carmel that the fight had become a goal in itself. I suddenly decided that I really did want a year of college. When I wrote to Father Wernert, his reply reflected the theology of the time: "Go now, you might lose your vocation, delay might not be wise." Even though I had the sense to question his advice, at this time and for many years afterwards, obedience and faith were synonymous for me. At seventeen I took his word as the will of God, and prepared to enter Carmel that September in 1945.

Only the final journey remained. Dad decided that he, Marge and I would fly to Indianapolis since I'd never flown before. I packed the few things I was supposed to bring, including my Bible in which was Mother's death card. Seeing it again with its picture of the Carmelite St. Thérèse, I wondered if Mother, in some way, was connected with my vocation.

After landing in Indianapolis we went to Carmel. Announcing ourselves at the turn,* we were directed to the enclosure door. We waited, uncertainly, for Mother Agnes and Mother Miriam. Finally with much key turning and rattling of locks, the door opened. They lifted their veils, for our brief goodbyes. I clung to my father. He held me tenderly, hoping to the end I would change my mind. I kissed him. He promised to write and to visit. We both tried to hide our tears as, at the enclosure threshold, Mother Agnes held out to me a small cross. "Kneel down," she said, "and kiss the crucifix."

As my story continues, I like to think it will be a lived, present-day interpretation, however imperfect, of the prayer charism of the Teresian Carmel. Many erudite commentaries have been written on the works of St. Teresa and St. John of the Cross, but there is something to be said for the lived experience, such as my own.

Part   II

VALLEY OF DECISION

2

POSTULANCY

They are not to use looking glasses,
nor are they to keep any curious
object....

Constitutions of the
Discalced Carmelite Nuns

CLAIRE AND I had hopefully peered through the lavender parlor windows during our first visits, but we could see only vague shapes of trees. My curiosity about the cloister had grown over the months. What was it like inside? When the enclosure door was locked behind me, I discovered to my delight that the monastery was just as beautiful inside as out. I was immediately aware of the same lavender light, the arched corridors, and above all, the same almost palpable silence. Meeting the community was a surprise — they were all so young! I had expected at least a few venerable old nuns, but decided no one there was more than forty, which proved to be right.

As it happened, I had entered a Carmel that had a unique
ancestry. Mother Teresa, our foundress, belonged to the famous
Seelback Hotel family in Louisville and was a deeply cultivated
person. She had died at fifty-four, nine years before I entered,
but had left behind a legacy of broad horizons. She had studied at
the New York Metropolitan Opera School and had also lived
abroad. Her wide circle of acquaintances included the founders
of *Commonweal*, a periodical edited by Catholic laymen, among
them Michael Williams. *Commonweal* had come to us from its
beginning. *America* magazine came from early-on, too, the gift
of Sister Anne's mother, Mrs. Clem, who felt we should not be
"utterly stupid." Sister Anne had entered from Washington in
the late 20's, against strong family opposition. (When her father,
General Clem, not a Catholic, came for his first visit, the turn
sister mistook him for the old umbrella man. She told him to
wait while she made him a sandwich. When she put the sandwich in the turn she suggested he could eat it on the front steps.
In a puzzled voice General Clem murmured, "I came to see my
little daughter.")

When I entered Carmel, I understood that I had come to
learn. My opinions and ideas, for the time, would be set aside.
People today express amazement and even horror at this idea,
but actually many professions demand a similar apprenticeship,
different, but the theory is the same. I was in Carmel to be
formed; my whole way of thinking, my clothes, my vocabulary,
my diet, were to change. Even my personal space had shrunk to
the size of a six-by-eight foot cell. When I entered the cloister I
became part of a sixteenth-century tradition. Here, the clock had
never been turned forward. Our life was, in many ways, a sort of
sublimated play acting. We have running water but acted as if
we didn't, using the bathtubs only once a week, washing in a
basin in our cells the rest of the time, eating with wooden
utensils, and sticking to many other centuries' old ways. In
novitiate, we happily accepted these customs, not necessarily

because we wanted them, but because they were considered part of a life of prayer and contemplation. Canonical comtemplative life at that time was found only in such organized structures. Consecrated virgins, living in the world under the jurisdiction of the local bishop, hermits, small experimental contemplative groups such as we have today, were unheard of.

Now I can see that many of my early difficulties came from an over-emphasis on my idea of the perfect — the idea of giving up *everything* for God. The problem, however, was that in my case, as a young, unformed person, I was trying to give God a maturity I didn't possess. This early training and concentration on the development of "Carmelite" morals and values later proved a stumbling block. Ordinarily in the first half of life certain developments of character and personality take place. In later life moral values develop and become clearer through experience. In my case, this process was reversed, for I first learned by rote, before any experience, certitudes which gave me a precocious system of morality. Only gradually and with much pain was I able to untangle this training and internalize it — breaking a mold I had thought held absolute truth.

My immediate Carmelite formation began the next morning. I was awakened by the harsh sound of a piece of wood forcefully striking wood. This was the clapper. Above this insistent noise, came the bellringer's* voice, "Come to mental prayer, sisters, come to praise the Lord." It was four-thirty in the morning. Being new I didn't have to get up until five-thirty. Lying on my straw-filled tick, I heard the bed boards creak beneath me as I turned over — too excited and happy to go back to sleep. My life, overnight, had become completely simplified. I was here where, for the past year, I had struggled to be. Family and friends, college — all, I thought dreamily, were a way of the past. I rejoiced in what I saw as the totality of my gift. I did not know then that the other side of this "Garden of Carmel" was desert.

My first experience of "desert" came shortly after my three-day formal adjustment period. It was the community retreat and I was sent to the parlor to speak, through closed curtains, to the Carmelite Father who gave it. For once in my life I had nothing to say. The weather was gloomy, I was already depressed, feeling I'd never become another Elizabeth of the Trinity, on whose life Father based his talks. "You must be looking forward to the feast of St. Thérèse, the Little Flower," he said. "No," I replied, "I don't much care for her — but I love the Spanish St. Teresa." "Humph," he said, and after a pause and some trivial exchanges, "Would you like to go to confession?" Astounded, I laughed and said, "Whatever would I confess? I've only been here a few days — there's not much wrong I can do here!" Silence. "You could," he said in stern tones, "start by confessing a lack of humility." I knew then that the Way of Perfection was going to be a much longer and harder haul than I had first imagined. How, I thought, can I be perfect, when I don't know what imperfections are? Externals at this point seemed terribly important to me. They were something I could understand and work on.

Determined to be the ideal Carmelite, "perfect," as described in one of our novitiate books, I absorbed every custom with a passion, although I often broke into laughter in the midst of carrying it out. We were, for example, to kiss the floor when the prioress passed, recalling in this act of faith, that superiors represent Christ. Unfortunately, this devotion was often marred by my giggles. Nothing had prepared me for this!

Kissing the floor was just one of many customs a postulant learned. "Recollection of eyes," and "keeping the silence," as we called it, not only in words but in movement, were also stressed. This was not for me an easy task, since every door in the monastery was thick solid oak with wrought iron latches. These latches, unless handled with extreme caution, would crash down with a noise like a pistol shot, the sound reverberating all through the vaulted corridors. Such noise was known as "breaking the silence," and was a fault. I began breaking records as I crashed from room to room.

All such customs were a special prayerful way of doing the natural things of daily life and giving them to God. Many of the customs we observed in the refectory were a 16th century inheritance, customs which for that century could be meaningful symbols because they could be interpreted and understood by the sisters' faith of that time. Refectory penances were a shock during my first months; stepping over sisters lying prostrate at the door, sisters begging bread on their knees, eating dinner on the floor. For our day, this had no cultural meaning of itself. We accepted the customs as having a religious significance. We ate in complete silence, listening to the reader of the week. Our wooden spoons and forks were the size of serving utensils, and we used tin cups for water. Our napkins served as placemat and bib. About one-and-a-half yards long, one end of my napkin rested on the table under my plate, then fell into my lap. I was shown how to pick it up and pin the other end to my dress. These napkins were washed only every two weeks and it didn't take long for their total whiteness to be splashed with beet and tomato tints. As each spot appeared, I used to think of my weekly confessions, starting out spotless . . . but so soon coming to grief.

Our diet was simple, since we bought only a few staples, like flour and sugar. Fortunately, we had a friend who was a dealer in wholesale produce. He regularly sent us his huge truck loaded with supplies of fruits and vegetables. A minor crisis would develop at times when we would discover five or six crates of radishes needing immediate attention, and crates of over-ripe bananas in a similar state. We had radishes mashed, fried and creamed; I preferred the banana bread!

Eating was only one element of our life in which customs played a part; responses to common courtesies were translated into a special language. Instead of "Thank you," we were to say "God reward you." "You're welcome" became "At your service." When you passed a sister in the monastery you said, "Praised be Jesus Christ," and she would conclude the greeting, "Now and forever." This is how the simplest things were used to lift our hearts to God. In later years, I thought them a kind of religious embroidery on the plain linen of life.

This new vocabulary was in the realm of the external and thus fairly simple to master. More difficult was being chaptered* or corrected for my "officiousness" and "levity." I was reprimanded for not practicing "poverty of time," for not using my time well. We had, for example, fifteen minutes between breakfast and work. In that time I was to visit the Blessed Sacrament, read a psalm in English to familiarize myself with the Divine Office (which was still said in Latin), read an excerpt from *The Imitation of Christ*, and, if I hadn't done it earlier, make my bed and fill my water pitcher. I realized how much all of these customs and rituals had become a part of me when, one day, a novice standing beside me at the kitchen sink, said, "God, I could use a coke and a cigarette, right now!" They were farthest from my mind! I was too busy trying to stay on the straight and narrow path in order to avoid further chaptering, and to become the perfect Carmelite I dreamed of being.

During the day, I obviously didn't have time to think about anything but each moment's obligation. My mind was filled, in the sunlit hours, with prayer, work, keeping the silence, and my search for perfection. When night came, however, I would lie in the hollow of my straw bed and give myself permission to remember . . . my father . . . home . . . my friends; I heard the music of our dances, wore the clothes I loved, and got in touch with that other part of me that still existed. It was my escape from the strain of perfection! Over the months, these images faded imperceptibly — their place gradually taken by all my new experiences. The bridge between my two worlds was still there, but, as my Carmelite identity became more real, I made the journey to my past less and less frequently.

St. Teresa wrote in our Constitutions that the nuns' work should be simple in order to free the mind for God. Our main work was baking altar breads. The novices helped with this task. We also made vestments, but the rest of our support came from alms and the kindness of others. Living expenses were minimal. Most of our food was donated, and doctors and hospitals gave their services without charge. Medicines were given to us by a family-owned pharmaceutical company in town. For us there was no such thing as health insurance premiums. Now these premiums take almost one-fourth of our earned income.

When I arrived, landscaping was in full force. Because it was expensive, we had decided to implement our dreams and do such work ourselves. First when I came, we built a small bell tower, next came stone patios, hermitages of St. John and St. Teresa and shrines. We all made an interesting construction crew at recreation time with our hemp sandals and our layered woolen garments even in hottest summer. We planted all our grounds, digging holes for trees and bushes. There were several acres of grass to be cut, too. Monday through Saturday, we worked hard. I counted the days till Sunday when no work was allowed. Sunday was a day just for extra reading and prayer, and walking in the enclosure we labored so hard on during the week. For my part, I especially looked forward to the extra time for reading.

Novices and postulants were given two books at a time, both selected by the novice-mistress. One was "light" reading — lives of the saints (which were often anything but light), and a second book covering prayer or some angle of moral or ascetical theology. Our light books were only for Sundays or the free evening hour between Compline* and Matins.* Reading was a special part of our formation* in Carmel. We had no formal classes for training postulants and novices, but the novice

mistress guided our reading individually. Our library held our
formation program. I felt we were fortunate in our Indianapolis
Carmel because Sister Anne made sure the library had the best
current theology books. We in formation, of course, had to wade
through many standard basic classics from the Summa to Tan-
querey before meeting such modern writers as Mersch and
Scheeben. I have always been grateful for these disciplined years
of reading, for later, when the renewal of religious life began, we
brought to our evaluations not only our lived experience, but a
reasonably solid theological foundation.

    We also had daily refectory reading at dinner and colla-
tion.*   This reading covered everything from the early martyrs
to the Renaissance, the missions, John Carroll and the American
church. Hearing church history read aloud day by day was easier
to digest, I decided, than reading hundreds of pages alone! I
vividly recall one biography we had. I was reader that week.
Weary of its length, excellent though the book was — I began in
a bored voice: "This is the continuation (sigh) . . . of the life of St.
Peter Canisius." Mother Agnes, whose table was close to the
reader's pulpit, tapped her cup smartly with her knife. "Don't
read like that," she told me. "Like what?" I replied with false
innocence. I knew that would not be the end of it. For me, the
weekly chapter of faults would undoubtedly hold a further
clarification on the virtue of not showing one's feelings. Besides
this reading there were community preached retreats, lectures,
and above all, monthly conferences by the Jesuits from their
house in West Baden.

    It was not until 1965 that I was to see a "live" view of history
— history in the making, very different from the refectory's look
to the past. For the first time, that fall, we borrowed a television
to see and hear Pope Paul VI address the UN. I watched in
fascination as he cried out, "Peace, peace, never more war!"
Later, someone gave us a TV set which we put aside "for special
church and state events." We watched the Democratic conven-

tion in Chicago and saw all the violence. I was deeply shaken. What a change from the hopeful world I knew after World War II.

Carmelite history and spirituality were high on our reading list. It was quite different reading St. Teresa, now that I was leading the very life she wrote about. Learning to live in community, which she mentions so often, was an education in itself, for we postulants came from various backgrounds, and had different ideas and expectations about what Carmel was to be. Along with St. Teresa, St. John of the Cross and St. Thérèse, (whom I had now come to appreciate vastly!) I read of the early mothers of the Order, Anne of Jesus, Anne of St. Bartholomew, remarkable women who risked everything to bring Carmel to France and the Low Countries.

Mother Miriam discovered that I read quickly, devouring books indiscriminately. This was considered "unmortified" — like gulping one's food. Reading was to be instructive — finishing one book to get to another was not at all the point. To cure my voracious appetite, most of my books had to be re-read, even the three tedious volumes of Rodriguez, *The Practice of Christian Perfection*. Written by an ancient Jesuit, it was meant to introduce the postulant to religious life. For me, the only bright spots in these drab pages were the stories about the Desert Fathers that Rodriguez used to illustrate his points.

I loved all Sundays, but especially the Sundays of the Advent, Christmas, Easter and Pentecost liturgical cycles. These cycles, along with the feasts of the Order, were often accompanied by octaves — or eight-day celebrations. They punctuated the year for us, giving some lightness and balance to our otherwise highly structured life. Each feast held its unique character and expression. Advent, for example, was a time of quiet waiting. Every evening the prioress carried the empty Advent crib of the Infant Jesus to a different sister's cell, for her day of recollection. We eight postulants and novices followed behind the twelve professed nuns, who wore their white choir mantles and black communion veils. I can still see the dim corridor, the candlelight and even now hear the Gregorian melody of "Jesu, dulcis memoria" which we sang as we walked in procession.

Advent days were cold and dark that winter. I always waited hopefully for the loud knocking in the radiators announcing that heat was on the way. Any warmth was short-lived because the monastery was built in the shape of a quadrangle, with windows lining all the corridors. The heat came up at five o'clock for evening prayer, and when we left choir an hour later for collation, the oak paneled refectory would still be warm. Each night, I felt an intense pleasure when after bowing to the cross behind the presider's* table, I went to the wooden bench at the end of the refectory where the postulants and novices were. We sat two at a table, steaming mugs of cocoa before us. A slow eater (I soon learned to be more prompt) I would peel my orange thoughtfully, relishing the tangy smell, wondering whether to eat all of my bread or leave some as reparation for my latest faults. Though dark outside, within we were bathed in warmth, light and peace. I listened contentedly to the reading from Father Faber's *Bethlehem*.

In spite of these beautiful traditions and rituals of the season — which I deeply loved — most of the time, spiritually, I felt cold and lost. My roots still clung to the past, but I knew I could never go back. I had changed. I had gone down the road too far to turn back. The old me was gone. But I couldn't seem to find the new me. In other words, I was having an identity crisis. St. John of the Cross had written on detachment that a bird, even though it be held by a slender thread, will still be unable to fly. I didn't then realize that attachments cannot be pried loose. They fall away only when, in the process of loving we find some thing, some One else, to love more.

Still, there were periods when I felt peace in the presence of God — and nowhere was that Presence more keenly felt than at prayer. At prayer I felt loved, understood, and affirmed in my vocation and in my ability to persevere despite my inner vacillations. At such moments I did know who I was and was sure of what I wanted to be. They were beginners' consolations which St. Teresa and St. John of the Cross reminded me would not last. I knew this was true, but I rejoiced in my good fortune of the moment and hugged these consolations to myself, hoping they *would* last. It was not to be. My feelings of love and devotion at prayer gave way to a vague spiritual emptiness, a restless searching for the remembered warmth of Christ's presence. Before long, I wasn't even sure that I had ever felt such happiness. Prayer brought only a heavy weariness filled with distractions. I saw myself as a dry river bed, once beautiful and filled with water, now barren and filled with stones. I knew the stages of prayer outlined by St. John of the Cross, but I could no longer believe they applied to me. My distractions were so mundane: daily small annoyances, no joy in my work. Interiorly, I now experienced revulsion for Office, the Stations, spiritual reading, all that I had once enjoyed.

I asked myself despairingly, "Is this the beginning of the Dark Night?" St. John of the Cross must have been writing for holy people — not me. I went to his teaching the way one would study a road map when lost. I re-read his words and looked again at the path of Nada, Nada, the path that led straight to the summit of Carmel. I studied the winding paths of the imperfect who reached the eternal banquet, but only slowly, by a much more round-about way. I understood the basic idea, that there were really two Dark Nights, each with its stages and never clear-cut: the active night of the senses and the active night of the spirit; the passive night of the senses and the passive night of the spirit. Some distinctions seemed clear to me. Active nights must mean that I had some choice about how to proceed, while

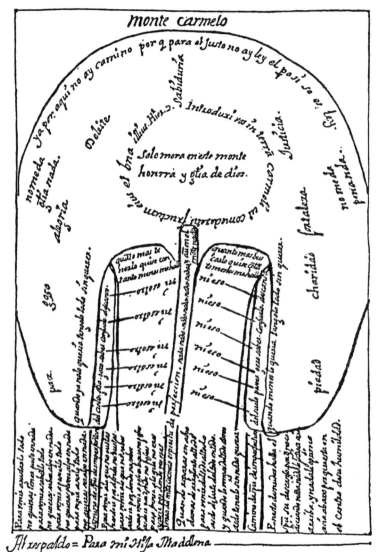

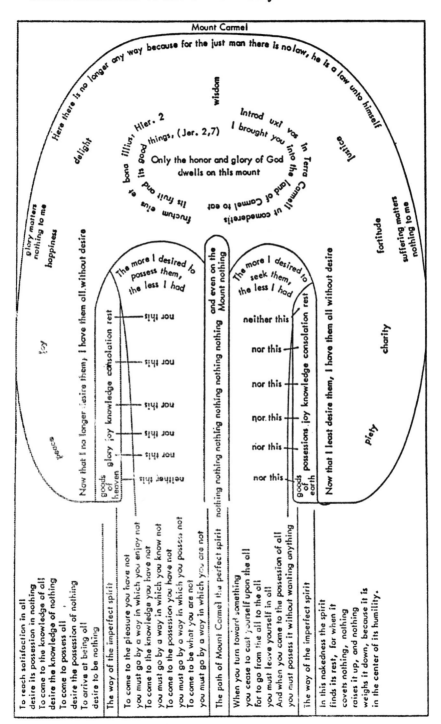

passive nights must mean that what God sent, I was to accept. As always, I wanted to know, to understand what was happening and regain control of my life. Until now, for me God had been clearly defined. He was "Carmelite" and asked me to practice prayer, silence and solitude, all of which I had enjoyed, feeling them sure signs that God and I agreed on my vocation. Was he now losing his identity or was I losing mine? Maybe he wasn't as Carmelite as I had first thought him to be; or maybe he had a different idea of prayer, silence and solitude. How could the unmoved First Mover change? I realized the answers to these questions could have serious consequences. I was out of my depth, in deep trouble, and too confused even to ask help in my spiritual distress. I wondered if other postulants were having the same problems. What were they doing about them?

Some of my anxiety was relieved by the nuns' light teasing about my receiving the habit. Symptoms of my spiritual blindness must not have been too apparent. When I received the habit, that would be a step forward. Then perhaps my spiritual life would return to normal.

I knew that no one was accepted for the habit without her formal petition and the vote of the chapter nuns. One gloomy day in February, while a red bird in the cedar tree called to his partner, I knelt in the chapter room to answer Reverend Mother's questions: "What do you ask?" "The mercy of God, the poverty of the Order and the company of the sisters." While the nuns put their black or white beans into the voting cups, I left the room and waited. It seemed forever before Mother Miriam came back for me. Mother Agnes announced I would receive the habit in May and my new name would be Teresa of Jesus. I was ecstatic — my prayer worries forgotten.

In March, my father and stepmother, Marge, stopped to see me for the first time on their way to Florida. I blurted out my news about the habit as soon as they sat down. Marge was pleased, my father tried to appear pleased. I saw unshed tears in his eyes. He tried to console himself that I at least would be safe in Carmel, for he knew that one of my close friends had just been seriously injured in a car accident.

A few days later I was thinking about this visit, while baking altar breads. Sister Mary came in to take my place, saying Reverend Mother wanted to see me. My first thought was that Mother Agnes had reconsidered accepting me. As soon as I saw her and Mother Miriam, I knew something worse had happened. I thought then that my grandmother had died, but it was my father. Mother Agnes told me Marge had just telephoned from the hotel in Florida. My father had died in his sleep. He was fifty-one.

Both Mothers tried to comfort me but nothing they said helped. I wanted to be alone and went to the choir to pray before a Presence suddenly become once again strange and distant, a Presence that had taken from me the person I most loved. I left the choir almost at once for the vegetable garden where the friendly mounds of sweet potatoes welcomed me. Wire fences holding last years' strands of vines were warmed by a pale spring sun. Could God let this happen, the loving heavenly Father that watched over even the sparrows? . . . I felt betrayed. Had I created an image of God to match my own needs for love and protection? As my image of God crumbled, I faced the reality of my father's death. Now I was an orphan. Sister Rose, who was working in the garden, came over to hold me and I sobbed out my sorrow to her.

The next days were interminable. When I asked about going to the funeral, I was told that if I did I would have to go through another postulancy. Actually, I had asked to go from a sense of duty. I felt no real desire to be at the funeral and see my father in his coffin; I wanted only to remember him as he had been in life.

Everyone who knew my father was stunned by his sudden death. In our family, where the grief was deepest, there was little we could share with one another. At such a time, what can be said? For me, eternal life, God, seemed far away. I wrote stilted letters to my sisters. Later Marge and Larry came to see me but, basically, we each had to live through our separate grief as best we could.

Days passed and I began to see more clearly the fallacy of my over-simplistic view of God. I didn't know God at all. Only with my father's death did I experience that dark apophatic knowledge of God which I had read about in St. John of the Cross; we know God by knowing what he is not. . . .

May the fourth, 1946, the day I received the habit, came bringing no joy. I was dressed in a borrowed wedding gown, of satin and lace, complete with a long train and veil. My family and many family friends came for my reception, but each person brought back wrenching memories of Dad. On a sort of white cloud of unfeeling I got through that day, and the two traditional visiting days that followed. Then my cloud turned to darkness, a torrential darkness holding grief and guilt. Did my coming to Carmel cause my father's death? I went over and over the arguments we had had about my entering. I console myself with the thought that my father had brought me to Carmel himself and only wanted my happiness. Years later in working on a spiritual journal I had kept for some time, it became clear to me that the grief I had carried for so long, like some sad, underground river, was that I had never had the chance to say goodbye to my father, to thank him for his love. I had never had the chance to say I was sorry for the pain I had caused him. If only, I thought, I could have said some of these things when he and Marge had come in March — but I had been too full of my own good news about the habit.

During the years to come, as I struggled to grow up, to grow free, I had to admit to myself that my father had been right: seventeen was too young for me to enter Carmel!

3

CANONICAL YEAR

*Meditating day and night
on the law of the Lord.*

*Rule of the
Discalced Carmelite Nuns*

My FATHER'S DEATH was like a
stone thrown through a web of illusion. I realized that God's love
did not protect one from pain and tragedy. I wondered what life
was all about; I wondered what I was doing in Carmel. But then I
found comfort in the thought that even St. Teresa had struggled
to resolve her way to God: ". . . although my will did not
completely incline to being a nun, I saw that religious life was the
best and safest state, and so little by little I decided to force
myself to accept it." I identified vividly with St. Teresa's attitude,
for I, too, was standing at crossroads, often working at cross
purposes, my feelings taking me one way, my mind another. An
extrovert in search of silence and solitude, I was understandably

47

confused. My novice-mistress, the one person with whom I could speak, often bore the brunt of my frustration.

As so often occurred, I was distracted from my spiritual ups and downs by community happenings. Just then we were experiencing that influx of vocations that occurred after World War II. Of sixty-seven Carmels in the United States more than half were founded after 1945. During those years, thirteen novices was not an uncommon number for us; there were seldom fewer than eight.

We were a cheerful cohesive group in my novitiate in those days. Our common call to Carmel was the main source of our closeness, but there were other factors as well. We were about the same age, most of us being somewhere in our twenties. Many claimed the midwest as "home," geographically, some from farms, some from cities. However, this commonality was tested not only by our different backgrounds, but also by our very different personalities. I can still recall us, seated in a circle at recreation, sharing together our lively, small world. Among the novices of those days were:

Ada Marie Fox from Dayton was the oldest in a family of five brothers. She was used to responsibility. Both Ohioans, we had mutual school friends. Conversation at recreation though was always general, so we could never share current news about our friends.

Rita Howard, her Indiana State Board examinations successfully passed, came to us fresh from St. Vincent's Nursing School. When we worked together she, with her brilliant dark eyes and hair, sometimes reminded me of a small song bird — a wren or a finch, so tidy and precise.

Jean Marie Hessburg was a bundle of energy, her long strong fingers always busy, as easy on others as she was hard on herself. She took her faults even more seriously than I did mine.

Rosemary Crump of St. Louis had worked as secretary for

Father Daniel Lord, S.J. The first-born of a large closely-knit family, she became our party organizer for the novitiate.

Marian Quinlan, a laboratory technician, had worked in Chicago at Michael Reese Hospital before she entered. Her vivid and amusing memories of hospital life and life with her sisters and brothers in Green Bay, Wisconsin, were always a welcome addition at recreation. Sister Grace, her sister, was one of our professed nuns.

Elizabeth and Marie Brady were another pair of sisters in our Carmel. I can see Sister Elia, quiet and calm with her horn-rimmed glasses and twinkly eyes . . . and Sister Marie with her round violet-blue eyes looking at the world with the heart of a poet. Both had been very active in Chicago's CISCA, a Catholic youth organization of that time.

Jean Alice McGoff came dancing into Carmel from college in Mexico City. We had been in grade school together in Cincinnati. Removing her earrings and high heels, she tucked her long black hair under her postulant's cap and set to work on "sainthood." With touching humility she tackled religious life, her *abandon* wonderfully contagious.

We all lived together as friends, very much like the first Christians, sharing everything in common. People might ask, "How could you be friends, how could you know each other when you didn't talk?" True, we kept silence during the day, but two hours of recreation, at noon and in the evening after meals, did provide a space for getting to know one another. Even though the topics were general, news of one's family, comments on current events, what we thought of Simone Weil's first book, did provide some insights about our individual attitudes and values. And there were articles from *America* which Mother Miriam read to us, and the poetry of Péguy or Alice Meynell, as we sat outside under the trees in the summer. During recreation a tiny clapper was sounded three times during the hour by the

Monitress, reminding us of the presence of God. We had customs for everything, some more relevant than others.

Was I lonely in what was basically a life of silence and solitude? An uprooted childhood gave me a certain emotional maturity. I didn't expect to find friendship, as such, in Carmel. Our way of friendship was spelled out in the Constitutions. I used to wonder why the Constitutions set so many limits to sharing and talking together. In later years, I realized that the "particular friendships" they mentioned referred to everything from a slight over-attachment to possible lesbianism.

Grates, grilles, rules, regulations and customs, for me, delayed my sense of personal responsibility and choice. I see now that the renewal and growth of the 1960s was the opening wedge to my deeper understanding of individual growth and maturity. It was a period of transition that was to prove painful and confusing for us all. As we grew older the challenges to life in common would become greater as the new emphasis focused more sharply on the individual and the individual's needs.

However, at this time in my religious life I found in the monastic silence a clarity of atmosphere, a deeper stillness, a place where I did not have to explain why I was happy or why I was sad. I could just be. I sensed the moods of others and they, too, were aware of my ups and downs. If I found a flower in my holy water font, I knew it was Sister Francis (Rosemary) — a holy card with a tiny note was Sister Teresa Margaret (Jean Marie) — all of us had our ways, our expressions of love and concern.

I thought the life of Carmel would remain unchanged, but our increasing numbers made a new foundation necessary in 1947. Still in the archdiocese, our new house was to be just seventy miles away in Terre Haute. Eight of the community were going. Arrangements for the new house were carefully planned. Together we prepared linens for the Terre Haute sacristy, woolen sheets and supplies of food. All was packed in huge crates. Hilarious episodes often resulted from the goodwill and limited experience of the novices. There was Sister Gloria and her crate. One of our most cerebral members, Sister managed to nail and bolt the sides of a crate with herself inside. Amid much laughter she climbed out by ladder.

That fall, amid tears and embraces, Mother Agnes and the sisters left us. I hadn't realized how traumatic that parting would be. We had become one family and now there was separation. In those days of absolute cloister, we thought we would never see each other again.

After they left, we settled back into our usual routine of prayer, silence and work. My work was clearly spelled out in the Constitutions:

"The year of the Novitiate, under the direction of the Mistress, has for object the forming of the mind of the Novices by the study of the Rule and Constitutions, by pious meditations and assiduous prayer, by learning what appertains to the vows and virtues, by exercises fitted for rooting out the germs of vice, controlling the emotions of the soul, and acquiring virtues."

All this in a year!

Novitiate life was simple in many ways. Simple as it was, it did not eliminate the frictions of daily existence. Take for example, mending. I thought it foolish to spend so much time on mending worn-out tunics. Yet Father General, when he came from Rome for a paternal visitation,* exclaimed with delight when he saw our mended tunics on the vestry shelf. "Ah, see these Americans! We talk about the wealth of our American Carmelites. They practice poverty just like our nuns in other countries." I was in a bad humor the rest of the day. Waste of time, I thought, too, as we checked over partially spoiled fruit in the kitchen, trying to save what we could. Actually, in time, it became all too easy for me to focus on these outward observances. I didn't grasp the whole-life approach of the Gospel which points to both outward and inward ways of humility and poverty. "Happy are the poor in spirit."

Engrossed in the life at hand, I gave little thought to what was happening outside. The world, the concept of a global village, was for me far into the future. I had only a vague interest in world news, but a number of the sisters found political issues and world happenings a real challenge. I simply wasn't interested, so engrossed was I in the minutiae of Carmel's life. But by the mid-1950s, Mother Grace initiated an important shift in our reading habits. She encouraged us all to read and form our own judgments and opinions, instead of being passive receivers. For a time each of the sisters had her own copy of *America*. We shared with one another at recreation our opinions about its articles — opinions, which I might add, clashed at times in a most interesting way.

Partly this early "separatist" attitude of mine came from the French school of spirituality I was reading at that time. It emphasized contemplative life as a transcendental relationship with God. This vertical model I took as my own. Still, through prayer and office, I was able to develop my spiritual oneness with the greater world of the People of God. This realization was deepened by many direct contacts with people through visitors who came to Carmel. Mail, too, arrived from far and near, letters asking prayers for many intentions. Later I helped answer mail. I still remember the weekly letters of one woman. She invariably stuck two quarters to her note with adhesive tape. Her intentions were always the same — her family, especially her son. She epitomized for me the faith of many. As I grew older, I began to feel that these friends were my extended family. Their hopes and anxieties became my own in prayer, and helped to rebalance my self-centered spirituality.

The twelve months of my novitiate year ended. (We all entered at different times so that we each had our own separate profession day.) Those twelve months had indeed brought stretches of desert, but I kept remembering "What makes the desert beautiful is that somewhere it hides a well." (St. Exupéry) To find this well was still my goal. Like the Samaritan woman I cried out to the Lord, "Give me this water that I may not thirst forever."

I was accepted for my three years of temporary vows. Monsignor Dugan, as the Bishop's representative, came to ask me whether I was in Carmel of my own free will, was I happy, and did I want to stay. (This was an opportunity for me to speak of any doubts I might have.) With all the brash certainty of youth, I said that I had none!

May the eighth, 1947, dawned bright and clear. The community gathered in the Chapter Room. Carrying my lighted candle, I knelt before the Prioress, hearing her repeat those words of the ancient formula:

Q. *"What do you ask?"*
R. *"The mercy of God, the poverty of the Order and the company of the sisters."*
Q. *"Are you resolved to persevere in the Order until death?"*
R. *"Thus do I hope and desire through the mercy of God and the prayers of the sisters."*

I placed my hands in the hands of the Prioress. That ancient gesture of obedience was for me and for all of us a symbol of faith. I then recited my vows.

"I, Sister Teresa of Jesus, make my profession of temporary vows for three years, and I promise obedience, chastity and poverty to God, to the most Blessed Virgin Mary of Mt. Carmel, and to you, Reverend Mother Prioress and to your successors, according to the primitive Rule of the Order of Discalced Carmelites and our Constitutions."

I lay prostrate as the *Te Deum* was intoned and the big bells of the monastery rang out. I thought of all the people I wanted to pray for. I thought of all the things I wanted to be for God . . . and of all the things I wasn't. I was filled with a new vigor and determination to go forward, but in my own way, toward my goal. I had yet to learn, over long years, that planning my own way to God was useless. The way to God is his way. My part, I found, was in the "waiting of attentive love."

4

TEMPORARY VOWS

*The Mistress of Novices is to teach them
how they are to act in times of
interior sweetness and in times of
spiritual aridity.*

Constitutions of the
Discalced Carmelite Nuns

THE "HOW TO" survival stage of
my Carmelite life was past. I could speak my faults with a fair
share of humility, get to choir on time without running, and in
general manage to keep my behavior in line enough to produce
only ordinary corrections. This breathing space made me feel a
great need to learn more about prayer — about why I had come
to Carmel. At first it had been easy to spend my prayer time
simply being in the presence of God. Next, as a novice I had had
to face the first prolonged period of dryness and distractions.
Now things were worse. My two hours of meditation seemed
endless. My mind circled here and there, like a hound on the

55

scent, always casting about for some new thought or idea, instead of learning to wait on God with "attentive love." Daily, we gathered in the novitiate for a short reading that served as preparation for evening prayer. Books could be used at prayer, but sparingly, as passing aids, and not as an escape from the discipline of prayer or, as the Zen school would say, from "sitting." In the face of prayer's empty dryness, however, I turned more and more to reading. One evening in choir, a pair of hands appeared over my shoulders and gently closed my book. Mother Miriam whispered, "This is prayer time, not the time for spiritual reading." The next day she spoke to me about dryness in prayer. Fidelity, she said, is being there for God — being open to his love even when it is unfelt. I agreed very much with her, and I wanted to make that attitude my own, but, as usual, my emotional reaction was anything but gracious. My moodiness and irascibility were in direct proportion to my difficulties at prayer. Going without food and sleep was one thing, but I never expected to go without God!

None of these problems, of course, was a surprise to Mother Miriam. She had spent years guiding sisters through spiritual deserts and around spiritual pitfalls. So part of learning to pray consisted in being taught what to do when devotion failed. We learned the Carmelite method of prayer, a very simple form of God's presence, but we were free to pray as God led us. We also learned to use the theory of other schools of prayer, should we so choose. Among my many efforts to solve my difficulties in prayer, I tried the Ignatian method . . . and then the French school of St. Sulpice as outlined by Cardinal de Bérulle and Jean-Jacques Olier. One thing, I found, always helped . . . those familiar words of St. Teresa in *The Way of Perfection*: "Daughter, as you are alone, you must look for a companion . . . and believe me, you should stay with so good a friend . . . nor will he ever fail you . . . He will help you in all your trials and you will have him everywhere."

I found great help, too, as I read the writings of St. Teresa's spiritual daughters. They brought a feminist perspective that balanced the views given from a masculine angle in conferences and retreats. St. Thérèse of the Child Jesus, Blessed Elizabeth of the Trinity, Edith Stein, a Jewish convert who entered Carmel and died in the Holocaust, all spoke to me of what it meant to be a woman in Carmel. (I was fascinated by the fact that Edith Stein had been Husserl's student and assistant in the field of phenomenology and immediately began to learn about philosophy!) It was fun, too, to read the lives of St. Teresa's early companions, such as Mother Anne of Jesus who founded Carmel in France in 1612. I was intrigued and heartened to find that someone as holy as she could write back to the beloved Spanish houses, "I eat all sorts of messes."

Another helpful guide was the wisdom of the great Irish Benedictine, Dom Columba Marmion. I took my copious notes from his books even to the baking room where I studied them while I worked. Marmion combined the values of monastic life and contemplative prayer, into a balanced synthesis of the cenobitical and eremetical. Parts of his novitiate life reflected my own early struggles, such as his outspokenness, for example. When asked by the novice-master what caused him most difficulty and made him suffer most, Brother Columba answered, "You, Reverend Father." (Speaking of this episode later, Marmion noted that being simple does not mean saying the first thing that comes into your head. Good advice for me!)

My prayer and its darkness seemed to be connected in some way with silence. Silence was a great stumbling block for me — unnecessary questions, jokes, "side remarks," laughter. I made an eye-catching small card, white, black and red, with just one word, SILENCE, on it. We often carried around a small holy card or a sentence to help our recollection. I carried my "SILENCE," but found it had a paralyzing effect on my sisters. After a short time, I laid it aside.

As the years went on, I came to realize that externals do not bring self-control. That comes from inner growth. At one time I had thought that "recollection" could be acquired by self-control, by ordering my outward activities. It was ages before I grasped the fact that there is a still inner silence that is a waiting of love, an attentive, interior life. The external silence of the monastery, a silence which I loved so much, was only an outward manifestation of an inner reality. In theory I was well aware that prayer time was not to be a separate time, but was to extend through all of life. In practice, my life remained very compartmentalized. In those early days I drew back from the thought of accepting a silence in the dark inner recesses of my own heart. I did not want to work with all my inner conflicts, noise and confusion. I was not yet ready to let go, to listen to what God was asking of me. Certain things I was ready to give him, but not all my attachments, my views, my attitudes. Silence, I dimly grasped, had to come from the inside out, from a detachment I was far from possessing. I tried various paths to that detachment which is really inner freedom. Every time we had a sermon or talk on poverty, I went through the items in my cell drawer and if I had an extra pencil, I gave it up. If I had two large safety pins to tie back my habit — instead of one — I turned one pin in to the Vestier (who hated to hear these conferences on poverty, knowing full well that she would get the results). Growing up spiritually had for me inevitable pitfalls, such as my scruples that confused real poverty with slightly ridiculous imitations. And I wasn't the only one! After such sermons, going down the novitiate corridor in the evening, I would see various small things set outside, now by one door, now by another. We all knew the ancient custom of the Desert Fathers. They never went to bed with anything in their cells that did not belong there. If they did . . . dread consequences could follow.

Life was not all spiritual. We were expected to know how to pray — but also how to work. As St. Teresa wrote, "We can teach the nuns how to pray, but God help us if they lack common sense." The expectation was that eventually every sister would be able to take her turn in the multitudinous offices of the monastery. This was achieved through a series of "assistant-ships." One of my first assignments was with Sister Mary in the sacristy. Sister was tall and thin, like those pictures of medieval saints I saw in my "Sunday" book. She worked with a clock-like precision which I found very edifying. Mother Agnes soon destroyed my edification. She scolded Sister for taking too long with sacristy chores. Fifteen minutes was the limit. For my part, I marked the missal for Mass and put the vestments in a two-way drawer that was pushed to the priest's side when he arrived. It was interesting to see how the various celebrants returned their vestments after Mass. Some simply dropped each piece in as it came off, some made an attempt to smooth over only the top piece, leaving the jumble underneath, and some, mostly Order priests, put the things back with perfect neatness.

I was assigned, too, to help Sister Rose in the kitchen. In the first place, I didn't know how to cook — which led to many adventures. Raised on a farm in Minnesota, Sister Rose was, for me, the epitome of common sense and practicality. Her bright blue eyes and pink cheeks, combined with a cheerful disposition, softened this effect of total efficiency. In the kitchen also were Sister Joseph from Kentucky and Sister Dolores from Chicago. Sister Dolores was a genius when it came to fixing things, be they egg-beaters or furnaces. I was never afraid to ask any of these sisters my endless — and sometimes mindless — questions: "What'll happen if I add the oil first?" "How do I know if it's done?" We took turns: some weeks Sister Joseph and Sister Dolores were in charge, some weeks Sister Rose and I schemed how to stretch the few small eggs our caretaker, "Mr. Z," brought over from his chickens. We never bought eggs; this was part of our practice of poverty. We made up for their lack by a whole list of "Black Fast" substitutes which included substitutes for milk, butter and eggs which were not used during Lent.

In time Sister Anne, as Sub-prioress, was to oversee my efforts at choir-cleaning. I was a bit in awe of Sister (there was definitely a hierarchy in jobs) because she took care of so many "important" things — the phone, answering mail and speaking with visitors. Naturally energetic, Sister Anne worked quickly — too quickly, in fact, for some! She was constantly being corrected: "Don't run, don't rush. . . ." Like a sprinkling of rain drops, these exhortations slid off the umbrella of her irrepressibly cheerful self. I admired her spirit tremendously. And yet, she puzzled me. I would have been crushed by such constant corrections. How did she manage to stay so cheerful? I realized later that she had the courage of her convictions and sometimes simply did not agree with certain views and attitudes and more or less ignored them.

In the midst of all this daily work, the Prioress and the three council sisters took care of the general business of the house. They managed such things as insurance, investments and building contracts. Important decisions were referred to the professed community for their vote. In an age when women had very little independence, we had a great deal of liberty, I felt, in running our lives.

All through these three years of my temporary vows, even as I fought the dryness and darkness of solitude, I was drawn to them with an inner conviction that, for me, they were the door to contemplative prayer. Alone, without false props to shore me up, I experienced a radical poverty: not just a lack of gifts, but a poverty of my very being. Strangely enough, this experience of my own nothingness grew in time to become an experience of freedom, "having nothing, yet possessing all things." I realized it was only at this level that genuine change could take place, a change that would come not because I wanted it, or even understood what needed to be changed in myself, but because then God was free to do his own work within me.

Today, it seems that people of faith everywhere are experiencing this call to an inner life of the Spirit. I believe their response to this call can open for them a way of peace and liberation through suffering, a way of freedom to love and serve. Some people are called to articulate this inner experience of prayer through social and political action, but many others are not. They will remain hidden, an unknown source of hope and strength for those who work on the cutting edge of our time for world transition and change.

5

FINAL VOWS

Stout in conscience. . . .

*Rule of the
Discalced Carmelite Nuns*

I MADE my final vows in the spring of 1950. Like my temporary profession, this ceremony was private. The public event was the reception of the black veil, symbolizing my new status. I was glad when my school friends arrived from Cincinnati, slightly late, due to a speeding ticket. They brought back to me happy memories of long summer days and that great celebration we had together shortly before I entered at the end of World War II. At twenty-two, after surviving a formation period of five years, I felt like an "old nun" as we playfully called the professed, and was happy to use my new-found maturity at the turn.

I loved the turn work. People came to us to ask for prayers and advice, or simply to share their joys and concerns. At first I found it difficult not to see the people that came. I was amazed, though, to find how much I could "see" with my ears. I used to wonder if our little black-curtained window at the turn gave people an added sense of security — rather like the atmosphere of the confessional. I was an expert in those days, able to find answers for theological problems, not only for myself, but for others as well. My answers were a bit too glib, a bit too black and white on the one hand and too ethereal on the other, "answers" which over the years quietly fell by the wayside.

The turn bell sometimes signaled a conference for the community, which meant that I made a breathless trip to find Reverend Mother Prioress and collect the nuns for the talk. Lectures were held in chapel. The doors and curtains in front of the grates were pulled back. Some priests were highly disconcerted by this arrangement for all they could see through the grates were two rows of black veiled figures seated on wooden benches running along each side of the choir. Their objections, however, were unavailing in the face of existing law. Through our thin veils we could see the speaker somewhat better.

One such important person who came was the Holy Cross Father, Michael Mathis. He was short with white hair, and wore steel-rimmed spectacles. Vitality flowed from him. He was the founder and director of the famous summer Liturgy Program of Notre Dame which still flourishes. Of all the sermons, talks, retreats and conferences we had, his came most alive for me. He was so possessed, so fired by the liturgy, that it was impossible not to catch his enthusiasm. For him, life and liturgy were one. He shared the story of his past with us in bits and pieces. One incident, which I never forgot, was the story of his missionary experience in India. He was there for nineteen years, when, as he put it, he was "kicked out by an episcopal boot." It was a devastating experience. Still much disturbed, one day not long afterwards, as he waited in the priests' parlor for a friend, he idly picked up a breviary from the table. The pages opened at Psalm

139: "You know me through and through. When I was being formed in secret, knitted in my mother's womb. . . ." He described how he was filled with an instantaneous understanding of God's providence for him and with the realization that nothing had been lost. Then, through a series of unexpected assignments, he found his second vocation, his apostolate in liturgy. I felt that the extraordinary power of Father Mathis' words were based on the fact that they came from a heart that had met and recognized the Lord "on the way."

For nine years Father Mathis was a significant part of our lives, introducing us to many fascinating visitors who were part of his summer liturgy program. One who came was the Jesuit, later Cardinal, Jean Daniélou who spoke to us on the *Canticle of Canticles* (the Song of Songs in the Old Testament). I found his French accent difficult to follow, but his enthusiasm and learning came through.

Father Louis Bouyer, of the Oratory, was another highlight, one summer. Father Mathis brought him down. What I found most helpful about this visit was that we became part of the discussion. They asked us what we thought about this point or that and what we felt was basic to liturgy and prayer. (We had made progress by then: the curtains were pulled, our veils were lifted and we were all in the speak room.) When Father Bouyer's book, *Liturgical Piety*, came out I felt a part of it because of his sharing with us. Father Mathis died in 1960, but I know his influence is still a part of me.

Father John Casey, a diocesan priest, was our first local guide to liturgy . . . and an ongoing source of diocesan news. He used first to look carefully over his shoulder into the public chapel and then say to us in low, confidential tones, "Now, you don't have to tell the Archbishop I told you this, but. . . ." Then would come some bit of inconsequential gossip to make us laugh. He had a great devotion to the early martyrs ("Poor Bibiana with her broken body"). I think, still, of his conferences when we celebrate the different feasts of the martyrs, like the "passio" of St. Ignatius of Antioch, longing to be ground like wheat by the teeth of wild beasts, to become the bread of Christ. He was dedicated to the rubrics! He told us about one Good Friday when he was Master of Ceremonies at the Cathedral. The church was supposed to be in complete darkness. Yet high up out of reach one light still burned. Ceremonies were halted. He sent for a ladder which was on top of a table. I could imagine him maneuvering his large frame to perch on the top rung. Teetering there, with one final breath-taking stretch, he extinguished the offending flame. Good Friday was a fitting climax to his Ash Wednesday episode. In his boundless enthusiasm, he had used ashes and holy water so generously that they produced a mild form of lye. The little servers went home with pink spots on their foreheads.

I lived in a world filled with rituals, symbols and signs, even as I realized that for the average person they no longer held deep symbolic meaning. Yet a definite sense of the sacred was created by these ceremonies, a sense that is still needed and desired. The challenge today, I think, is to find meaningful symbols and a ritual at the parish level that will reflect the sacred for our own times.

If liturgy was my first love, a close second was philosophy. I met the classic Greek philosophers weekly when Monsignor Doyle came from Marian College up the road. Once I understood the philosophical terms, they helped me to analyze and clarify my own thinking, both in and out of prayer. Previously, I had more or less skipped over such words in my reading, "intuiting" their meaning. Yet the frustrations of everyday life sometimes got through to me and all philosophy failed. Then I wondered if I had been simply taking refuge in an intellectual fortress.

On such days I felt very lonely, a loneliness I could never understand, for I "possessed" so many answers! Worse, I had a growing intuition that I would continue to be lonely until I came to a real acceptance of the solitude I had chosen. Slowly I came to know that only in solitude does one come face to face with one's self. Only then does one find "the face I had before I was born." Sometimes I discovered a temporary distraction from my loneliness. On Sunday I treated myself to Georges Rouault's *Miserere* with its beautiful, bold engravings. I copied and kept some of the pictures' captions. Two of my favorites were a crucifixion with "Obéissant jusqu'à la mort et à la mort de la croix" — "Obedient unto death, even the death of the cross" — and a picture of a mother and child with "Il serait si doux d'aimer" — "To love would be so sweet." I pondered, not exactly with regret, but with a certain wonderment, the thought of the children I might have had, of being loved by one special person. Another "escape" was Jacques Maritain's *Creative Intuition in Art and Poetry*. Four lines that he quoted there from T.S. Eliot's "The Hollow Men" made me realize that life itself is lonely and that loneliness is an existential condition of us all.

> At the hour when we are
> Trembling with tenderness
> Lips that would kiss
> Form prayers to broken stones.

Through such experiences of mind and heart, the choice of my own vocation with its vows of poverty, chastity and obedience, became progressively clearer to me. Erik Erikson defines intimacy as "the capacity to commit onself to concrete affiliations and partnerships and to develop the ethical strength to abide by such commitments, even though they can call for significant sacrifices and compromises." I came to realize that the struggles of these early years had a positive as well as a negative effect. I discovered through experience that, while stages of growth are imperative, there is always more than one way to grow! Admittedly, my way was more complicated than most because of the life itself. But because our God is a God of wholeness, I found in the end that our rigid schedule became a tool of growth for me. Its discipline demanded that I learn to change mental gears, and get on with whatever duty called at the moment. No matter how I felt about it, how much I wanted to linger over my books, procrastination was out. On Sunday, when the big bell boomed out for Vespers, I would close Rouault's book with determination and set out for choir. Once there, I could feel Sunday's quiet and peace settling again in my heart as we recited "In exitu Israel de Egypto . . ." "When Israel came out of Egypt." I was "Israel" and I had found a home.

My final profession was a profoundly moving experience. It was the Holy Year of 1950. It seems to me that Holy Years now hold less significance. Then they were great occasions with the impressive opening of St. Peter's bronze doors and all the accompanying pomp and liturgy. Today, along with everyone else, I am overwhelmed by the tremendous explosion of change that has come upon us. Our world finds itself in a painful period of transition and fear. I see how power, success and nationalism have come face to face with the nuclear age, humanity's encounter with St. John's Dark Night. I ask myself, what lies beyond?

Our own life of Carmel knew great changes the year of my final vows. Pius XII's directive on religious life, *Sponsa Christi*, was promulgated. I was delighted with its emphasis, for I saw that for the first time, the federation of autonomous monasteries could become a real possibility. If our Carmels federated, I knew it would mean our meeting and working together. I happily read the cautious Roman phrases: "Although, as a rule, federations of monasteries are not imposed, nevertheless, the reasons which would recommend them in general, could, in particular cases be so strong that, everything considered, they would be deemed necessary by the Sacred Congregation." This document was primarily directed toward the needs of contemplative houses in Europe. Their poverty in the aftermath of World War II was extreme. Supported for the most part in the past by their endowments, many European contemplatives were now destitute, needing food, clothing and medical supplies. In Indianapolis Carmel we had always had to support ourselves, so for me the idea of remunerative work was not the issue, but rather that federation would mean a communion and union of us all.

My dream, though, was not to be reality. The idea of federation failed to take hold. Through questionnaires and meetings the sisters began to see some of its undesirable consequences. As I look back today, two issues seem to have been the stumbling blocks, self-government and autonomy. Every Carmel is juridically and financially on its own. Although following the same Rule, each house develops its own family spirit and customs. I realize now that centuries of virtual isolation couldn't be overcome so easily in our monasteries in this country. We were not prepared for so radical a change and our problems were not those of Europe. We had had, though, the experience of meeting together and sharing our ideas and hopes for the future. For me it had been a tremendous experience when we held the first regional meeting of seven Carmels at our Indianapolis monastery in 1954. Fourteen sisters came as representatives. These regional meetings were climaxed by one national meeting in Philadelphia at Eden Hall in 1955. They voted for federation. In the end a national federation was never achieved. Still the idea of federation was always waiting, like a seed, quietly biding its time.

The meetings of the 1950s, from their early beginnings, had had for our Indianapolis house, as well as for other Carmels, many constructive results. On the practical level I was delighted to have a summer habit and tunic that was much lighter in weight, though still wool. When I worked outside with the sisters we all could have a second tunic and extra baths. My monthly "List of Leaves"* was curtailed. I could drink water outside of meals without asking and keep mending materials in my cell. I could write to my family and need not ask for soap or toothpaste. All was included when I said, "I beg to renew my List of Leaves."

These early changes were vitally important to me even though they involved neither the Rule nor the Constitutions. I began to worry; were we losing some of our Teresian tradition? Was it right? I realized gradually that living tradition is only preserved by being lived out and constantly reinterpreted.

After the "List of Leaves" and other small adaptations in our external schedule and dress came the first great liturgical changes for Holy Week and Office from the Generalate. I liked the new Holy Week and Easter Vigil Services better than the old ways — and the fact that they were in the vernacular. What a relief to read the Office lessons in English without worrying about the Latin pronunciation! I could see the Mass, for the black curtains were now pulled back. From a rather foot-dragging approach to change, I began to see that change was not only possible, but in most instances, highly desirable. Some changes were easy, some were hard. What I have discovered is that change is like a road, never finished, but always part of the journey.

Part   III

MIXED BLESSINGS

6

CROOKED LINES

God writes straight
with crooked lines

Portuguese Proverb

THOUGH I WAS UNAWARE of it, in the midst of all these small changes, one great change was imminent, the Reno foundation. For all religious groups new and larger novitiates were being built, seminaries were expanding, and the influx of vocations seemed limitless. When we first asked our Archbishop Schulte about the Reno foundation, he had agreed. He realized we were turning away vocations because of a lack of room. Later, he called us. He had looked up Nevada in the Catholic Directory. Was it prudent? Was it wise? Nevada had only 500,000 people in the state. It was still mission territory. Bishop Dwyer of Reno reassured our Archbishop that the Reno people would support us.

We all volunteered for this western mission, including myself. I wasn't keen on the idea but was still on "the most perfect thing" track. I could think of nothing harder than leaving my beloved Indianapolis Carmel. Little did I know that, due to poor health, fourteen years later I would be in Reno, too.

Bishop Dwyer arrived for his first visit to Indianapolis shortly after the final foundation agreement. I caught only glimpses of his red cape as our Archbishop took him through the monastery. Usually, visitations, such as they were making, are official episcopal visits to a religious group. I suppose this one was really a semi-visitation to show the Bishop of Reno how things were done.

Eight sisters were going to Reno. Because we had all offered to be part of the foundation, it was decided to divide gifts and talents as evenly as possible between the two houses.

The foundation papers came that August (1954), on the eve of the Feast of Our Lady's Assumption. I found this separation a difficult time, just as I had before when the Terre Haute foundation was made. We had so many shared experiences — so many downs — so many ups! The new foundation, working for it and praying together, seemed to me to create even closer bonds between us.

Mother Angela, our Prioress in Indianapolis, was to lead the foundation to Reno. Sister Anne was to be Sub-prioress. They both flew to Reno to find a suitable house. Ultimately, they discovered a chiropractor's old building that could be renovated.

The first group of four, Mother Angela, Sister Rose, Sister Marian, and Sister Joseph, left in August on the New York Central. Sister Aimée, Sister Mary Thérèse, Sister Elizabeth and Sister Anne followed a week later. We still have in Reno the receipt for those eight August train tickets, a grand total of $448.29! They had a wonderful welcome in Reno. New friends made them at home, rallying to their aid. The nuns' first house still stands at 829 North Virginia Street, a few blocks from the famous Club district. In the night the sisters could hear the huge interstate trucks passing by and the staccato click of high heels.

We learned, to our distress, that the Reno Carmel was plagued, almost from the beginning, with health problems. First one sister and then another went to St. Mary's Hospital. Dr. Noah Smeroff, a newcomer like themselves in Reno, took them all under his care. Another new friend, John Cavilia, started them on their printing venture, which is, even now, our main support. John taught Sister Marian to run the ancient Multilith we had acquired. The "print shop" was an old shed behind the house, so old it was built with handmade nails.

Vocations to the Reno foundation, for one reason or another, were not working out. Echoes of comings and goings came to us. They had been in Reno just two years when their youngest novice, Sister Marie, died from leukemia. They asked us for help. Again, we all offered ourselves — I felt more trepidation than the first time! After a community discernment process and in view of the Reno needs, Sister Michael was chosen to go for a year. In the end she remained as a permanent member. Sister Michael and I had been novices together. Another gap in our Carmelite family.

After the sisters left for Reno, the fifteen of us who were left carried on the regular schedule once more. I began to notice when we were outside that Sister Marie would sometimes quietly leave and go indoors. I can still remember how pale she was, one summer day, as she pounded an iron stake with a sledge hammer to make holes around a tree for fertilizer. Suddenly she laid down her tools and left. None of us realized that she had heart trouble. We knew, though, that she was not strong and her work load was lightened. Her health problems increased, however, and shortly after the Christmas of 1955 she was taken to St. Vincent's Hospital for examination. We learned only then that she had a serious heart condition, with, at most, only a year to live. We were stunned. Sister was thirty-three. We moved a hospital bed to the first floor so that she could be near us as we worked. An electric stair glide was installed on the choir steps. Sister Rita, our nurse, was the infirmarian.

May came — the cherry tree blossomed near the bell tower — the roar of race cars trying out at the Indianapolis Speedway drifted over the walls. Peacefully and calmly, Sister Marie waited. At noon recreation one day, some of us were scoring cardboard for altar bread boxes. Sister, delighted that she was well enough to be with us, was sitting beside me on a high stool, her feet tucked into the lower rung, sleeves rolled up, enthusiastically wielding a heavy cardboard scissors. Suddenly, without a sound, she slipped from her chair. Blood from a gash on her forehead made a scarlet pool on the gray terrazzo floor. I had never seen a person die, but I knew immediately that she was dead. One of us ran to call the doctor, another the priest. We carried her to her room. I couldn't seem to hold her. The weight was death's reality. Father Courtney arrived and anointed her. I remember gathering around the bed as we all recited the prayers from the Ritual. As I stood there, facing the window, I saw a sky as blue as only Indiana skies can be, dotted with puffy white clouds. I knew, with tremendous force, that while her body lay so still — so dead — before me, somewhere she was singing, somewhere, I *knew* she was with God, near us still, happier than she had ever been in time.

We took turns keeping vigil. Flickering candles around her coffin were the choir's only light. I knelt for my watch by her bier. Her life seemed to pass in review before me. Gifted in many ways, she had worked closely with a Jesuit, Father Stenson, in Chicago at CISCA, a Catholic youth organization. She was sometimes clumsy with manual tasks, famous for dropping things. We never realized why. What do some things matter, I thought. Clumsiness, talents, all that doesn't count. Like the Fox in Saint-Exupéry's *The Little Prince*, I realized, "It is only with the heart that one sees rightly." She was a great person who loved much. I determined to work harder on my failings. I remembered Mother Miriam's reply to my confident statement, "I have a strong will. When I want to do something, just watch me!" "Just watch you," she said, "just get out of your way!"

The experience of Sister Marie's death reinforced those early lessons of detachment I had learned from my parents' death. I was soon to learn still more about detachment through my own ill health. The strange aches and pains, the exhaustion I had been having became more severe. Feeling very unmortified, I told Reverend Mother Prioress about these problems. Since neither of us understood what was happening, we both agreed to wait a while. The pains increased. A doctor came to examine me. I lay in bed, feeling foolish; probably nothing was wrong. He moved my arm up and down a few times, asked some questions, and then went over and leaned against the door frame. He said to me, and to the Prioress and infirmarian, "Given your age and your symptoms, I would say that you have rheumatoid arthritis. This disease is incurable and nothing, really, can be done about it. However, there is a new drug. It won't cure you, but it will relieve the pain." Next day, I began taking cortisone. Satisfied that he was the expert, the three of us felt it unnecessary to ask further advice. Rheumatology, at this time, was relatively unexplored.

"Keeping the regular observance," well or ill, was vital to me. To "carry on" was a precious tradition in Carmel — exemplified by past and present saintly Carmelites whose death notices we read from time to time. I felt I should be like them.

Cortisone lessened the pain, but still, I felt ill and more and more discouraged. In the early morning when the pain was worst, I would sit in the darkness on the edge of my straw mattress, helpless tears running down my face. How could I put on the heavy habit and manage the tiny veil pins I could no longer hold? The sisters would have been delighted to help me, but I was stubbornly determined not to say anything. St. Teresa had said, "When the illness is serious, it proclaims itself." I took this very literally. Never having been ill before, I had no experience to draw on. Had I been older, I hope I would have had more sense. As it was, none of us knew anything about rheumatoid arthritis. Neither I nor my superiors realized that this type of arthritis would move slowly, causing various complications, with good days and bad. For one thing, like so many people, we didn't know the difference between my rheumatoid arthritis and osteoarthritis — the "wear and tear" disease. It was 1957. I was thirty then. It was twelve years after I entered.

Why did I have arthritis, I asked myself. Was my life in Carmel making me ill? Or was this caused by some genetic factor, or emotional state? Not knowing any answers and able to keep "the regular observance," I did not ask for further help. God, I thought, would give me the grace I needed. As yet, there were no great visible effects except that I was thin and pale. Spiritually, I was immersed in my latest motto from *Liturgical Piety* by Father Bouyer, "Tota Laus Mysterii" (Wholly in praise of the Mystery). Those words were like music to me. "The mystery, first of all, is God Himself, in his deepest nature so unsearchable to our reason. . . . 'Christ in you, the hope of glory. . . .' " Those words summed up my deepest beliefs and gave meaning to my pain. I felt this illness was a test of the reality of my faith and my prayer life. I wondered if all this was part of the passive purification St. John of the Cross speaks of. He definitely mentions illness as one of those things we cannot control — one of those things we are called to endure.

Plagued with constant pain, however, inwardly I began to rebel — and, in rebelling, felt guilty. Week after week, I confessed to "a lack of faith, for not accepting God's will." Our Franciscan confessor, Father Philip Marquard, was a man of tremendous common sense and compassion. He had been our confessor for many years. After months of hearing me repeat these words, one day, he said tentatively, "Is there any particular problem connected with this lack of faith that you would like to talk about? I don't want to intrude, but if there's something we could discuss. . . .?" My words poured out in a torrent: "I have so much pain I can't handle it. I'm impatient and angry and irritable. I know that if I had more faith, I wouldn't feel this way — I would see the pain as a grace." I burst into tears. I knew that if this illness was a test — I had failed it badly. Father sat quietly on the other side of the grate. When my sobs subsided, he asked, "Have you seen a doctor?" I told him the community doctor had examined me. I waited for a lecture on accepting pain. Instead, he simply said, "You should see a specialist." Easier said than done, but eventually I saw Dr. Robert Healy, an internist who suffered himself from a severe disease that impaired both his speech and movement. I at once felt at ease with him. A gentle, kind person, he asked many questions, and listened carefully. When I told him I took aspirin, he asked how many and when. I answered three in the morning, three at noon and three at night. He asked what I took them with. Shocked at the thought, I answered, "Nothing, we have a fast." "You must *never* take aspirin on an empty stomach. You will *not* take aspirin on an empty stomach. I'll see to that." And he did.

Looking back, I realize this doctor's kindness opened a window for me. I became aware that keeping external regulations like the fast was not necessarily wisdom — and, more importantly, I learned that passivity was not necessarily a virtue. Dr. Healy referred me to a competent young orthopedic surgeon, Dr. Irvine, for my X-rays. Though in constant pain, I never had considered myself actually ill. On my second visit, Dr. Irvine put the film of my right hand in his X-ray holder. "Here," he said, taking a pencil and tracing the outlines with the eraser, "Here where the cartilege should be smooth and round, yours is eaten away. The first joint of your index finger is hanging by a thread." He had many different X-rays of joints, all of them showing serious deterioration. I was in shock and in tears as I sat in the musty taxi on the way home. The bright spring green I had noticed going to my appointment, was now without any message of hope. Through my mind kept running the thought, it is too late, the damage is done. Had I brought this on myself by my mistaken idea of virtue? I was angry, angry with myself, with the community, with God. With my vivid imagination, I saw my body disintegrating, and me inside it! Would this have happened to me if I had not entered Carmel? And then, again, I wondered if so much damage could have been prevented. It is a date I have never forgotten, April the twenty-eighth, the feast of St. Paul of the Cross.

When my condition was realized, help was mobilized. One of the doctors arranged for me to have physical therapy at the hospital across the street. I was told that the caretaker's wife, Mrs. Zurschmied (whom I was very fond of and who took all of us to such appointments) would take me. My rebellion in full swing, I violently objected to her help this time. Did I need a companion to cross the street? A cab was suggested. I argued it would look foolish to any cab driver to take a fare such a short distance. Weary of my outrageous insistence, the Prioress sent me on my rebellious way — alone. Wearing the one brown mantle we used when we went out, I was given the gatehouse keys.

My spirits lifted as I bolted and locked the door behind me. The fall day I drove to Carmel with my father came vividly back to mind. Spring was now alive again. As I walked down the long drive the wind whispered through the pines, red birds chirped and fluttered. I walked slowly, savoring my new sense of freedom. A moment of panic seized me as I passed through the front gate and left my quiet monastery grounds. Cars streamed by. I hadn't expected such heavy traffic on Cold Spring Road. The moment of panic passed and I safely crossed the street. Annoyed by my lack of confidence in such an ordinary situation, I thought in disgust, "So much for cloister!" For months Dr. Martella's physical therapist worked with me, showing me how to protect my joints from strain, how to sit, how to walk. (I had the habit of walking with bowed head. I thought it helped recollection. The therapist said I walked like a chicken.)

In my fear, I had an exaggerated need to know all the ins and outs of my illness, but my efforts backfired. One book on arthritis had alarming pictures. The book's final statement — "For rheumatoid arthritis, the cause is unknown and treatment uncertain." My world became a narrow corridor. I hated being sick, I hated the pain. All my thoughts centered on myself and my health. Gone was my abandonment to Divine Providence — my idea of suffering in silence. I was back with the toads in St. Teresa's First Mansion. In my turmoil I remembered how she had explained that the soul doesn't move in orderly fashion from one mansion to the next. In this castle, she had written, the rooms are connected and the soul moves back and forth, sometimes forward, sometimes regressing. . . . I regressed! As my pain grew, so did my depression. Just as in dying, denial, anger and bargaining were part of my struggle to come to terms with pain. Only I knew I *wasn't* dying. I knew my life was still very much ahead of me. I believed, interiorly, that my illness and pain were a polishing process (as St. John of the Cross calls it) not a punishment. But I adjusted slowly, gradually, very gradually, as I tried to let go of my anger and frustration. Meantime, I took refuge in reading, especially scripture and the lives of the saints who had suffered with Christ. At prayer I learned a lot about simply enduring, simply being there, giving myself to God as I was, usually feeling a miserable heap, and learning to be comfortable with the misery.

Our retreat in 1963 was given by the late Father Walter Ciszek, a Jesuit, who for years had been a prisoner in a Russian concentration camp. I thought him a saint! (Actually, his cause* is now being discussed.) I asked him about faith — how had he kept his in such a dreadful situation? At the close of our visit, he wrote this sentence for me on a holy card: "Faith is Christ's life in us."

My health more or less stabilized and, later that year, I was made novice-mistress. This was something I very much appreciated because in order to prepare for daily novitiate, I was given extra time for reading and study. Best of all, I went to the first national meeting of Carmelite prioresses and novice-mistresses at De Matthias Hall in St. Louis in the summer of 1965. This meeting was organized by a much loved Carmelite, Father Thomas Kilduff, who was for me and for so many others a moving spirit in the nuns' renewal. He offered his affection, his support and his guidance in helping us assume a greater responsibility for our contemplative lives. We came to St. Louis by car — by jet — from the East and West coasts for our six-day meeting. I was impressed by the big jet plane — so different from the plane I'd taken to Carmel twenty years earlier! At De Matthias Hall we each had our own room. I found mine luxurious compared to our small cells. It had a bed with a mattress, a desk, a comfortable chair and lamp, bookshelves — I hadn't had such conveniences for a long time. Father Charles Schleck, from Notre Dame University, gave the first talk in the large meeting hall, "The Value of Systematic Theological Instruction in the Cloister." I can still feel the excitement I experienced at his words. Somebody important was saying what I had always believed in. I was one of the five sisters who took notes and wrote reports covering assigned sessions. Often tired (I still had an active case of rheumatoid arthritis), I nevertheless managed, with my sleeves rolled up, to bustle about, typing papers, comparing notes and vastly enjoying all the new ideas.

I thought, at the meeting, that we had agreed on renewal. However, like the bishops after Vatican II, it proved difficult for the participants to share their experience when they returned to their monasteries.

Encounter magazine began life as a trial issue produced at Reno to distribute at the St. Louis meeting. As editor, I typed all the talks and reports for publication, a demanding and challenging labor. *Encounter*, we all hoped, would be a means to continuing our St. Louis dialogue. Though *Encounter* is no more, in its day it had a tremendous impact.

I was delighted to see the thrust of the St. Louis meeting recognized and supported by the Vatican Council when it opened just three months later. It was the fourth and final session under Pope Paul VI. I saw in print in the *Decree on the Appropriate Renewal of Religious Life* that outmoded customs and habits should be updated, the very things we had all debated among ourselves in community and at meetings. This document gave shape and form to all our former timid adaptations. Big changes began in Carmels which took Vatican II as a formal directive. There was a new interpretation of cloister and we took down the grates in the chapel. We got driver's licenses and went out to vote and shop. None of this happened overnight. It was a long and painful process of discernment. I know renewal is still not over. Obviously we contemplative nuns face increasingly complex situations given our cultural and moral world of today.

I threw myself whole-heartedly into editorial work for *Encounter* after the St. Louis meeting, but I soon began to experience more arthritis problems, along with diminishing strength. I went to the doctor, who declared, "If you don't do something about your arthritis, in six months you'll be in a wheelchair." Surgery was his choice. Mine was to accept the Reno community's offer to come to their Carmel in the dry and sunny West. Once in a different climate I felt my arthritis would improve. Requesting a transfer to Reno was one of the most difficult decisions I ever made, but my options had run out. After months of seesawing back and forth, I wrote Sister Michael, warning her that I was quite handicapped, could work little and my health was expected to worsen. She answered, "Come." A generosity typical of the Reno community!

I flew into San Francisco's huge, crowded terminal in August of 1968. I felt exhausted and out of place in my long brown habit. I had left Indianapolis on a morning flight. It was now evening — a long day. Unable to find the Reno connection, I wandered around in a daze, at last finding my plane with little time to spare. In Reno, Mrs. La Fond, a close neighbor, met me at the airport. Although I felt at ease with this pleasant and attractive woman, I could hardly believe what was happening to me as we drove through Reno. I felt myself in an alien world.

Washoe Valley is surrounded by high peaks. Even to reach the monastery, Our Lady of the Mountains, we drove in low gear up a steep, narrow, twisting road, so different from the long level approach at Indianapolis. But when I finally arrived at Carmel's entrance and embraced the sisters after our fourteen years' separation, I realized, with a tremendous sense of joy and relief, that I *was* home! I was very excited, my tiredness forgotten. Here were all the people I had lived with for so many happy years before we had to part. There was Sister Michael, my novitiate companion; Sister Rose, as joyful as ever; Sister Elizabeth, now finally professed — they were all the same special people. I soon discovered our two communities were still very close in their thinking and their dreams. Carmels are not blueprints of one another: each house eventually creates for itself a special family spirit, even though following the same rule and constitutions. Reno, too, in the West, had adapted to a new environment. I saw, in the smaller monastery, friends who took care of the chapel instead of caretakers. Everything was on a simplified scale.

Their recreation room and its wall of windows facing east was my favorite place. Holding my breath, I often stood at those windows, at night recreation — watching the enormous jets float down from the mountains to the airport's landing strip, lights blinking in the dark. Another treat was sitting by our corner fireplace, watching the flames die down to embers. Most of all I enjoyed Hans, with his perfect manners and his beautiful coat, ranging from golden brown to black — the perfect German Shepherd. His pedigree credited him as descended from the famous line of Rin Tin Tin.

Though the Reno community was not Indianapolis, a large library and conferences were still a high priority with them. I liked the fact that Carmelite Fathers came as visitors and for retreats. Other lecturers came regularly from the Jesuits' University at San Francisco. Though Reno was not exactly "on the way" to anywhere, it was amazing how many visitors we had. The ones I best remember are the Jesuits, Daniel Berrigan, David Stanley the biblical scholar, and Alonso Schökel from the Biblicum in Rome.

I spent a lot of time that fall, sitting in the sun, in a garden chair — a blanket tucked around me, against our chilly Washoe Zephyr. I watched the poplars turn golden, the funny robins stuffing themselves on the red pyracantha berries, becoming too inebriated to fly, the tiny hummingbirds, the orange and black butterflies and the fat quail promenading along our cedar enclosure fence. I saw all about me the beauty of our mountain valley. I loved to watch the changing light, brightening first one peak and then another. At night, I found the stars really are closer in the West! All this rest with warmer and drier weather did relieve some of my pain, but a change of climate was not enough. I spent the next year-and-a-half in and out of hospitals in Cincinnati for reconstructive surgery and physical therapy.

Mine was not the only transfer. This era of renewal was a period when many Carmelites changed monasteries. Since Vatican II, with its emphasis on the individual, many, for the first time, began to evaluate their own needs and ideals. I found that those who transferred had hopes for everything from a deeper solitude to greater opportunities for education and service.

In Reno, we welcomed four sisters from Pewaukee, Wisconsin, and four from Morristown, New Jersey. There were, first from Pewaukee, Sister Mary, a surgical nurse; Sister Teresa, an expert printer; Sister Candida, wonderfully capable; and Sister Joan Meyer, our Golden Jubilarian who died a few years later. Not much later, our four sisters from Morristown arrived. An artist by profession, Sister Marie Celeste's designs brought new life into our print shop. Sister Maria and Sister Patricia ultimately followed each other as Prioress. Another Sister Joan (Antisdale) who died in 1983 at the age of 85, was dearly loved. Reno's forward-looking group was soon growing together into a single community and I loved being part of it.

After many months in Cincinnati, I returned to Nevada, hospitals behind me, ready for my Second Journey in Carmel. Extensive remodeling of the house had been done while I was away. This was an alternative to building the fourth and last wing of the monastery, which we felt would be superfluous given our small numbers and our desire for simplicity. I had a bright new office for *Encounter*. Two large windows looked out on grass and trees and, beyond our grounds, stretched Nevada's sage and tumbleweed.

That spring, on my recollection day, I took my first small walk. To my amazement the desert ground was carpeted with tiny pink phlox, and desert violets. In such barrenness, so many exquisite flowers! Holding my cane, I leaned on Sister Teresa's arm as we walked. We followed a rough, stony path to the irrigation ditch. Propped against the base of a crooked poplar tree, whose trunk leaned over the swirling water, we ate our bread and cheese. The silence of the land was intense, broken only now and then by the song of a lark.

I began to sleep better at night. My appetite improved and I gained weight. Some mornings, I didn't even need help to get dressed. I went regularly to the Dominicans' St. Mary's Hospital for physical therapy. There a competent Peggy Heidrich listened patiently and dispensed much wisdom along with her range-of-motion exercises. But as I grew better, I began to dread these visits. I had had my fill of hospitals, even as an outpatient! Peggy suggested swimming would be my best therapy.

Myra McCue, long a friend of the community, hearing this, welcomed me to her class in aqua-aerobics at Moana pool. Sister Betty regularly drove me there since there was no public transportation. (This car, a Ford Mustang, a gift, gave rise to a wonderful myth. Nuns in a distant Carmel, we heard, were convinced that the Reno sisters were riding a real horse through town!) At first, I could hardly manage to get down the pool steps, but soon I swam whole lengths. My range-of-motion increased and I became more confident about my chances of avoiding a wheelchair.

The most disappointing thing about my 1969 stay at Holmes University Hospital in Cincinnati, was missing the Seminar for Contemplatives. It was held in Maryland, in August, at the Jesuits' Woodstock house — quite a contrast to the famous New York Woodstock Festival with the same name and dates. Carmelites made up one-third of the members of the meeting, among them some of my closest friends who were in the core group preparing the agenda for the meeting. I had very much wanted to be part of this. The sisters in Reno sent me, to my delight and excitement, an electric typewriter. Typing with my right hand — my left was in a huge cast — I wrote letters to Sister Constance in Baltimore, and to many other friends. My reward was the mail the young nurse's aid cheerfully delivered to my room each day. Mine was a corner room that looked out over a roof into a brick wall. I relieved its monotony by decorating its walls with my favorite posters. Dr. Evelyn Hess, on her daily rounds, always found my bed covered with papers and myself busily pecking away. Trying to hide a smile, she said severely, "Sister Williams, you must learn to rest. Do you have to be always working?" I really did work all day. My novice work ethic was still operative. Night was my time for prayer and solitude. I slept lightly and was often awake. Against the muted background of night traffic and hospital sounds I found a contemplative solitude of stillness and prayer.

As I sat in bed reading the news which Sisters Jean Alice and Rose Page sent me about the coming meeting, I had plenty of time to think. I knew we were part of a Church which was coming to life, even as the exodus from religious life continued. I studied the preliminary questionnaire which asked us all, "How do contemplatives see their life of prayer — their role in today's Church?" Rumors were rife that a new document on cloister was on the way. I wondered if it would prevent the nuns from going to Woodstock? Thirteen years had passed since a broader approach to cloister had been mapped out by the Vatican document, *Inter Cetera*. It had been followed by Paul VI's equally broad document, *Pastorale Munus*. And then I thought with satisfaction, for the present day came Vatican II's decree on religious life, *Perfectae Caritatis*. I knew its words by heart: "The papal cloister . . . is to be retained. Still, it should be modified according to conditions of time and place, and outdated customs done away with. In such matters, consideration should be given to the wishes of the monasteries themselves."

I soon learned about a letter from Cardinal Carberry, who was then head of the Pontifical Commission for Contemplative Nuns in the United States. He sent it to all contemplative houses in this country. "Recently," he wrote, "notices have appeared in the press of attendance of contemplative religious at symposia, workshops and similar gatherings which may have serious effects on their contemplative vocation. In the name of the Pontifical Commission, may I respectfully request that our contemplative religious abstain from attendance at such gatherings while the question of their renewal and adaptation is under study." When the nuns who were planning the meeting read Cardinal Carberry's letter they consulted various canonists. They were advised to continue with their original plans since the purpose of the seminar was to foster contemplative life. Cardinal Carberry's request was partly based on the fear that the mixing of various contemplative groups would lead to a loss of their individual charisms. An even greater fear was that the sisters would take renewal into their own hands.

Actually, as far as the loss of my own Teresian charism was concerned, when I went to such meetings later on I found my own Carmelite vocation more clearly delineated for me as I talked with others. There is a way of knowing who one is, I found, by experiencing what one is not! I came to a deep appreciation of the rich heritage of the courageous women I met, among them, Poor Clares, Benedictines, Trappistines, Dominicans, Sacramentines, Passionists.

And then, in the midst of this gathering of hope and prayer at Woodstock, the cloud burst. A Latin copy of the rumored document, *Venite Seorsum*, arrived. It was immediately translated. Signed by many of the nuns, a letter was sent to Pope Paul VI expressing their concern about the backward thrust of the document. When I read it I was hurt and confused by what seemed the obvious lack of trust that it implied. Some of its more archaic points were: two locks, still, on the enclosure door; a book to sign when leaving the cloister; the TV, if there was one, to be kept under lock and key. These were small in comparison with its final declaration that any recent changes, which had been directed by Vatican II, were to be evaluated against the norms of this document. Vatican II had told us to renew and update. Now we heard that we must undo what we had done, a pattern of control that always seems to reappear when too much initiative is taken by any individual or group. I had chosen to lead a contemplative life. I was in Carmel because I wanted to be there — not because of two keys, grates or grilles.

It was a help to all the contemplatives gathered at Woodstock to be there together when *Venite Seorsum* arrived.

Sisters were there, too, from the Leadership Conference of Women Religious and from the Center for Applied Research in the Apostolate. People like Sister Marie Augusta Neal and Sister Mary Agnes Cunningham who had worked for many years with contemplatives were present to help sort things out. This meeting, it seems to me, just because of the intrusion of *Venite Seorsum*, was able to reach beyond its original scope and find a new clarification in what was essential in our life for the Church and what was merely accidental. As Joan Chittister, O.S.B., once pointed out, "To the Roman mind, the function of law is to define the ideal. . . . To the American mind . . . the function of law is to define the normative." I well remember the conference when I heard Paul Boyle, C.P., say that canon law is meant to be interpreted, not followed literally. These words changed my approach to the future.

For me security in the past had been in knowing right answers — never mind asking right questions. "Experts" in every field could be consulted: theologians, canon lawyers, scripture scholars, someone for everything! It never occurred to me (or to most of us then) to look at our own experience and ideas. That would have been "suspect." It surprised me to see how simple it was to absorb this new emphasis and return to the outspoken ways of my youth.

At the end of the Woodstock meeting, thirty sisters were appointed to help form the permanent group which became known as the Association of Contemplative Sisters (ACS). I have been an active member of ACS for many years. The Association's special purpose is to intensify and develop a life of prayer for all, seculars as well as religious. ACS has given members a unified voice to express their views. One such instance took place during 1985 in Chicago. Sisters Jean Alice and Helen Weir represented the Association before the Bishops' Committee preparing their pastoral on "Women in the Church and Society."

The Sisters spoke on the role of contemplative women in the Church today.

Sixteen of our Carmels had never given up hope of federating. In 1970 the Baltimore Carmel made one of the last attempts to federate. They asked Cardinal Sheehan to carry a petition to Rome seeking permission to take steps toward establishing a federation. A rescript finally came from the Generalate through Father Christopher, the Carmelite Provincial. In three months, Sister Teresa Hahn and I were on our way from Reno to a meeting at Marriotsville, Maryland. After having missed Woodstock, I was especially happy to be one of the forty-three delegates. It was fun meeting these sisters from so many different houses. I was part of the small group that worked on our statement of purpose for our new Carmelite Communities Associated. It was a reality. Three more Carmelite federations were later formed.

The present Carmelite General suggested that a national federation might be the ideal. Personally, I believe that an umbrella organization to include individual Carmels as well as existing federations might be more successful. After forty years of religious life I see the cyclic patterns of the past still being relived. Yet I know that from the past the future flows, always filled with hope.

EPILOGUE

It is advent now — a fitting time for memories to pass to the future. Like the earth and its seasons, the liturgical year has come full circle. Last night, snow fell and today, after Mass, I put on my boots and walked down to the cemetery. There I stopped for a space by our three graves to ponder those smaller cycles of timelessness, of death and resurrection. Beyond the cemetery, another ragged path meanders through the scrub. I scuffle along, dragging my feet, amazed as always by the sheer number and variety of the stones and the green plants still able, because of sun-warmed rocks, to exist in the snow. I reach the wooden shrine that shelters our large carving of Christ seated on a donkey — Christ facing this time, not toward Jerusalem, but toward Reno's downtown. I search for a place to sit and find an old stool, made gray and rickety by summer suns, that offers a dry spot and is strong enough to support me. I watch the red-tailed hawk, who makes our ground his preserve. He circles, swoops and sails to the north. Westward, the splendid snow-covered bulk of the Sierra Nevada stretches out, primal and untouched.

I have come to this solitude to think about some specific questions that have developed while I have been writing this book. But the silence overpowers me and I feel a mental blankness in the face of nature's grandeur. My eyes are drawn over and

93

over to the outline of Mt. Rose, to its slopes and valleys, its tree-lined peak. Slowly, as the chill creeps into my toes and fingers, my questions return. Questions, I realize, that have in these later years gone beyond my early search for "perfection" and my current questions about the future of contemplative life. I have been called out of myself, beyond the insularity of the rules and regulations of my early years, to a realization of my connectedness with the world about me. This broadening of my mind's borders has come about in great part through two friends of my community, living in different parts of the world: through William Johnston, a Jesuit who has lived in the Far East for some thirty years; and also through Stephen Judd from Maryknoll who serves in Peru's Altiplano. Over the past three years Steve has shared with us his Third World experiences. Knowing both people has been an education for me. From Steve I heard in my heart the questions of the Third World; from Father Johnston I learned the richness of Eastern thought and prayer. I wonder, as the sun gathers strength and warms my head, how contemplative life meets East and West. I ask myself, can contemplative life really be in dialogue with the Third World, the Orient and every culture? I am convinced it can because contemplative life, of its very essence, transcends and embraces the culture and peoples of every land.

Recently, through Steve, I have begun to grasp the complexities of the North/South dialogue. I find that the hardest questions for me come from the South, from its poor, its hungry. Between these questions and my reading of liberation theology, I have begun to think more deeply about the bridge that links my life to the missions. Actually, the tie between Carmel's prayer and the mission world is not new. St. Thérèse, the French Carmelite nun (together with St. Francis Xavier as patron) is patroness of the missions. I believe it is not a question for us of developing a new apostolate, but rather of listening to what this dialogue between contemplation and mission said in the past, and what it now says today. To do this, I think we need a new hermeneutic, a hermeneutic of retrieval, of recovery, to formulate and possibly redirect our horizon of service. As Jack Welch said to our Carmelite nuns, "You need to name your experience, to speak what you hear in the dark." These words often came back to me as I struggled to write my story.

I believe that the future of contemplative life will become clear only by experiment and experience. Experience, however, is a two-edged sword. I myself find an almost daily tension between the framework of our old structures and the ongoing demands of dialogue with the broader and changed community, let alone the Third World. Yet, even as I question this tension, I know it is a necessary part of our continuing process of self-discovery and self-definition. These kinds of dialogue with the poor of the Third World, with the poor of our own cities, are just one of the challenges contemplative life faces today.

As I sit here under the blue Advent sky, I think of certain areas of commonality that already link the poor of South America with contemplative life: simplicity of lifestyle, respect for the earth, community living, Marian devotion. Our Carmels also share with the campesinos a growing awareness and trust in our common experience of reaching out and trying to direct our own lives. Another similarity that might seem far-fetched is possible martyrdom. However, dying to oneself in religious life became known as a white martyrdom, after Constantine recognized Christianity and actual martyrdom ceased. Religious life became a martyrdom without blood. The first to embrace white martyrdom were the Desert Fathers (whose lives I savored as a novice), men and women who went to the desert, not to escape from the world, but to die to themselves and live to God in prayer, fasting and penance. As their numbers grew, so did rules and regulations supposed to protect the original charism of the founders of the desert way. I agree that all this commonality with the poor, in one way, is only surface. The poor have no choice. I only hope that my choice of a contemplative lifestyle, of the desert, expresses my solidarity with the poor even if it is expressed more by an interior attitude than by visible appearances.

My own life in Carmel offers a good example of how, like the Desert Fathers, too much institutionalism can work to the detriment of charism. We were first asked in 1966, by the Order, to undertake the revision of our Constitutions, an undertaking that has continued for the next twenty years. This was why I was deeply relieved when, in 1977, the Declarations, the updated version of the Constitutions, arrived from the Carmelite General, Father Finian. Our Carmel and many others happily lived with the Declarations for the next five years. At the end of this period 85% of our sisters, world-wide, voted for their permanent acceptance. However, a small group of Carmelite nuns carried their strong objections to Rome. The Holy See bypassed the right of a religious order to write its own Constitutions. The Sacred Congregation for Religious (SCRIS) took over from the current General, Father Philip, in 1985. A new commission was assigned once more to revise our sisters' Constitutions! I was amazed that the acceptance of so many was put aside for a few objectors who sincerely identified with the old ways of discipline and dress. They alone had been heard, not the others. The future remains unclear to me, but here we are.

I know these old ways. They are as familiar to me as the path I walked this morning. Now I dream of a new path that will lead to the heart of the mountain where it is always Advent. Where Christ both hides and reveals himself, where the hawk will come full circle and be at rest.

> I see him, but not now
> I behold him, but not near.
>
> Numbers 24:17

Advent, 1987

GLOSSARY

BELLRINGER: A sister appointed weekly to ring the bells for various monastic functions.

CAUSE: The first stage of the process required for canonization.

CHAPTER OF FAULTS: Weekly gathering when the nuns spoke their faults or were corrected for failing to observe the Rule and Constitutions.

CHAPTERED: A correction taking place at Chapter.

COLLATION: Evening meal during times of fast.

COMPLINE: See Divine Office.

DIVINE OFFICE: Official, daily prayer of the Church made up of Psalms and Scripture: included the Hours of Prime, Terce, Sext, None, Vespers, Compline, Matins and Lauds.

FORMATION: Period of instruction before final vows.

HABIT: Distinctive garb, often based on the dress of the ordinary people at the time of the foundress — for Carmel's St. Teresa, the sixteenth century.

LIST OF LEAVES: Permission for ordinary necessities asked of the Prioress each month.

LITURGY: Formal worship of the Church and the formulas set forth for public praise.

MATINS: See Divine Office.

MONASTERY: From the Greek word, Monas — alone — a convent of nuns or brothers.

NOVICE: One who has received the Habit but not made vows.

PATERNAL VISITATION: A non-official visit of a religious superior to a convent.

POSTULANT: One in the first stage of religious life.

PRESIDER: One who officiates at community gatherings.

PROFESSED NUN: One who has made final vows.

RETREAT: For an individual nun, a period of intensified solitude and prayer — a community retreat included conferences.

SCAPULAR: Part of the religious habit consisting of two long panels falling over the shoulders, back and front.

SEAL OF CARMEL: Depicts Mt. Carmel, surmounted by a cross, in the center, three stars in the field — the arm with flaming sword carries the legend from Elijah: *Zelo zelatus sum pro Domino Deo exercituum.*

THIRD MANSION: In her book *The Interior Castle*, St. Teresa describes seven mansions or stages in the spiritual life.

TURN: The revolving barrel with an open side that could be turned to the visitor to give or receive what was placed there.

VEILING CEREMONY: When the white veil of the novice is replaced by a black veil signifying that a nun has made final vows.

VOWS: The traditional components of religious life — poverty, chastity and obedience.

BIBLIOGRAPHY

ABBOTT, WALTER M., S.J., ed. *The Documents of Vatican II.* (New York: America Press, 1966).

ALONSO-SCHÖKEL, LUIS. *The Inspired Word: Scripture in the Light of Language and Literature.* Trans. by Francis Martin. (Montreal: Palm Publications, 1965).

BALTHASAR, HANS URS VON. *Elizabeth of Dijon: An Interpretation of her Spiritual Mission.* Trans. and adapted by A.V. Littledale. (New York: Pantheon, 1956).

BERGSON, HENRI. *Matter and Memory.* Trans. by N.M. Paul and W.S. Palmer. (New York: Humanities Press, 1911, 1970).

BERRIGAN, DANIEL. *The Bride: Essays on the Church.* (New York: Macmillan, 1959).

BOFF, LEONARDO. *Jesus Christ Liberator: A Critical Christology for our Time.* Trans. by P. Hughes. (Maryknoll, NY: Orbis Books, 1978).

———— *Saint Francis: A Model for Human Liberation.* Trans. by J.W. Diercksmeier. (New York: Crossroad, 1982).

BOUYER, LOUIS. *Liturgical Piety.* (Notre Dame, IN: Univ. of Notre Dame Press, 1955).

CARMELITES OF EUGENE, OREGON. *Elizabeth of the Trinity: A Name, a Presence, a Message.* (Carmel of Maria Regina, 1980).

FABER, FREDERICK WILLIAM. *Bethlehem.* (London: Burns & Oates, 1960).

GUTIERREZ, GUSTAVO. *Liberation and Change.* (Atlanta: John Knox Press, 1977).

———— *The Power of the Poor in History.* (Maryknoll, NY: Orbis Books, 1983).

———— *A Theology of Liberation.* (Maryknoll, NY: Orbis Books, 1973).

———— *We Drink from our own Wells: The Spiritual Journey of a People.* (Maryknoll, NY: Orbis Books, 1984).

HAHN-HAHN, IDA VON. *The Fathers of the Desert.* Trans. by Emily Bowden. (London: Burns & Oates, n.d.).

IGNATIUS LOYOLA, SAINT. *The Text of the Spiritual Exercises of St. Ignatius.* Trans. from the original Spanish, 4th edition, revised. (Westminster, MD: Newman Book Shop, 1943).

JOHN OF THE CROSS, SAINT. *The Collected Works of St. John of the Cross.* Trans. by Kieran Kavanaugh, O.C.D. and Otilio Rodriguez, O.C.D. (Washington, DC: ICS Publications, 1979).

JOHNSTON, WILLIAM. *Christian Zen.* (New York: Harper and Row, 1971).

———— *The Still Point: Reflections on Zen and Christian Mysticism.* (New York: Fordham Univ. Press, 1970).

MARITAIN, JACQUES. *Creative Intuition in Art and Poetry.* (New York: Pantheon, 1953).

MARMION, COLUMBA. *Christ in his Mysteries: Spiritual and Liturgical Conferences.* (St. Louis: B. Herder Book Co., 1924).

———— *Christ the Ideal of the Monk: Spiritual Conferences on the Monastic and Religious Life.* (London: Sands & Co., 1926).

MEYNELL, ALICE. *The Poems: Complete Edition.* (London: Burns Oates and Washbourne, 1940).

NEVIN, WINIFRED. *Heirs of St. Teresa of Avila.* (Milwaukee: Bruce Publishing Co., 1959).

PÉGUY, CHARLES. *The Mystery of the Holy Innocents and Other Poems.* Trans. by P. Pakenham. (New York: Harper & Brothers, 1956).

RODRIGUEZ, ALPHONSUS. *The Practice of Christian and Religious Perfection.* (Dublin: James Duffy & Co., n.d.).

ROUAULT, GEORGES. *Miserere.* (London: Trianon Press, 1950).

SAINT-EXUPÉRY, ANTOINE DE. *The Little Prince.* Trans. by Katherine Woods. (London: William Heineman, 1958).

TERESA DE SPIRITU SANCTO, SISTER. *Edith Stein.* Trans. by Cecily Hastings and Donal Nicholl. (New York: Sheed and Ward, 1952).

STEIN, EDITH. *The Collected Works of Edith Stein, Sister Teresa Benedicta of the Cross, Discalced Carmelite.* Edited by Dr. Lucy Gelber and Romaeus Leuven, O.C.D. Trans. by Josephine Koeppe, O.C.D. (Washington, DC: ICS Publications, 1986).

TERESA OF AVILA, SAINT. *The Collected Works of St. Teresa of Avila.* Trans. by Kieran Kavanaugh, O.C.D and Otilio Rodriguez, O.C.D. (Washington, DC: ICS Publications, 1985).

THÉRÈSE OF THE CHILD JESUS, SAINT. *The Autobiography of St. Therese of Lisieux.* (Washington, DC: ICS Publications, 1975).

THIBAUT, RAYMOND. *Dom Columba Marmion: A Master of the Spiritual Life.* Trans. by Mother Mary St. Thomas. (St. Louis: B. Herder Book Co., 1949).

THOMAS À KEMPIS. *Of the Imitation of Christ, as trans. by R. Whytford, anno 1556.* (New York: Duffield & Co., 1909).

WEIL, SIMONE. *Waiting on God.* (London: Collins, Fontana Books, 1969).

Periodicals:

AMERICA. America Press, Inc. 106 West 56 St., New York, NY: 10016.

COMMONWEAL. Commonweal Foundation, 15 Dutch St., New York, NY: 10038.